Cake Plates

CAKE

Barbara & Jim Mauzy

Schiffer Publishing Ltd ®

4880 Lower Valley Road, Atglen, PA 19310 USA

Designed by Bonnie M. Hensley
Cover design by Bruce Waters
Type set in Bitch Cakes/Lydian BT

ISBN: 0-7643-2015-7
Printed in China
1 2 3 4

Published by Schiffer Publishing Ltd.
4880 Lower Valley Road
Atglen, PA 19310
Phone: (610) 593-1777; Fax: (610) 593-2002
E-mail: Info@schifferbooks.com

For the largest selection of fine reference books on this and related subjects, please visit our web site at www.schifferbooks.com
We are always looking for people to write books on new and related subjects. If you have an idea for a book please contact us at the above address.

This book may be purchased from the publisher.
Include $3.95 for shipping.
Please try your bookstore first.

You may write for a free catalog.

In Europe, Schiffer books are distributed by
Bushwood Books
6 Marksbury Ave.
Kew Gardens
Surrey TW9 4JF England
Phone: 44 (0) 20 8392-8585; Fax: 44 (0) 20 8392-9876
E-mail: info@bushwoodbooks.co.uk
Free postage in the U.K., Europe; air mail at cost.

Dedication

This book is lovingly dedicated to Jim's mother, Jean S. Mauzy. Jean is an inspired chef able to concoct masterpieces from seemingly nothing. But more important than that is what a loving mother, mother-in-law, grandmother, and great-grandmother she is! A truly sweet person deserves a book on a sweet subject. Yes, Jean, light on the chocolate. How about pistachio?

Acknowledgments

The Cover

Don't you love the cover? Again we thank Bruce Waters for a wonderful design. But what about the tantalizing cakes? Those cakes, and many more, are baked daily at **Silk City Diner**. "It's Diner Time" any day of the week when you stop in for a great meal followed by an unbelievable dessert baked right on the premises. What a perfect cover they have given us by donating their scrumptious delights. You can have some for yourself the next time you come to Adamstown to shop with us. Stop in at 1640 North Reading Road (that's Route 272, the same road on which you'll find us at Renninger's, just two miles south), Stevens, Pennsylvania. 717- 335-3833.

The Content

Some really wonderful people contributed a huge assortment of fabulous pieces for this project. First of all, Walt and Kim Lemiski earn the prize for most pieces and most miles. They arranged to transport gorgeous glassware from the Dufferin County Museum & Archives located in Ontario, Canada – all of Chapter Four! Beyond that, there was all the hunting and finding Walt did to fill in the gaps enlisting friends, the DCMA, and simply searching. Not to be forgotten are other helpful friends, many of whom have contributed to other books we've written. We so appreciate everyone's enthusiastic participation: David G. Baker, Brenda Beckett, Bob & Cindy Bentley, Wayne & Jean Boyd, Ted Bradley, Sylvia A. Brown, Wes & Carla Davidson, Tom Dibeler, Charlie Diefenderfer, Les Fawber, Michelle Frazier, Barbara L. Jaquett, Janice Johnston, Kathy McCarney, Neil McCurdy, Doris McMullen, Dave and Jamie Moriarty, Norma Peacock, Carl L. Pellham, Lorraine Penrod, Bill Quillen, Paul Reichwein, Julie & Jim Retzloff, Michael Rothenberger, Aimée Schuld, Marie Talone, Susan S. Waters, Brian J. Wing. If anyone is overlooked it is not due to a lack of appreciation. Thank you all so very much.

About the Book and the Prices

The main focus of this book is on cake plates and carriers one might find in today's marketplace made in the late 1920s through the early 1960s. Wherever possible, manufacturer identification and information is provided, and a history of some of the manufacturers of cake carriers is included in Chapter Seven. A sampling of serving pieces is also contained within this book, provided as an addition to this subject and not intended as a comprehensive reference.

Values are shown as a guide rather than as firm prices and these values vary immensely according to the condition of the piece, the location of the market, and the overall quality of the design and manufacture. Condition is always of paramount importance in assigning a value. Prices in the Midwest differ from those in the West or East, and those at specialty shows will vary from those at general shows. And, of course, being at the right place at the right time can make all the difference.

Neither the authors nor the publisher is responsible for any outcomes resulting from consulting this book.

Contents

Introduction

These words are among the first spoken to our children. We may not read the same fairy tales generation to generation and we may not sing the same tunes, but a handful of rhymes easily survive and pass from mother to child countless times. Why this one?

What is the affinity we hold for dessert that even led many to adopt the mantra, "Life is uncertain, eat dessert first?" Perhaps these words explain (or at least justify) our preoccupation with sweets: "Everybody has a 'sweet tooth' of considerable size. As a nation we Americans consume more sweets in every form than any other group in the world - and that is a tribute, not a criticism. We need more sugar, because individually and collectively we move faster and farther than any other national group. Sugar in every form is what feeds that dynamic energy."[1]

Having said that, and agreeing on some fundamental level that we all need to feed our dynamic energy – after all this is a tribute to our intrinsic nature, this book focuses on our love of cake. We clap a rhythmic verse with our babies about this delicious treat (staple?) as we have been baking and serving cakes for generations. Our language is replete with references to this satisfying creation. "Would ye both eat your cake and have your cake?"[2] "Yes! Yes!" we heartily reply. We WOULD have it and eat it!

First, however, we need to create it and serve it. Going back to the late 1800s the women of Grace Methodist Episcopal Church in Utica, New York offered these sage words:

Hints on cake making:

- Flour should always be sifted just before using.
- Baking powder should be thoroughly mixed with the flour.
- Select the best of material for cakes. Always cream the butter and sugar first, then add the yolks of eggs, milk, and last the flour and whites of eggs.
- Yolks and whites of eggs should always be beaten separately.
- Remember that sweet milk and baking powder go together, and sour milk and soda.
- Cake should always be beaten - not stirred - in this way the air is driven out of the batter.
- Never ice a cake hot, and let layer cakes get nearly cold before putting together."[3]

Once created, there is the ritual of serving. Cake reigns so supreme in the scheme of desserts that it has earned a podium, a presentation so grand it is physically elevated above all other foods and even the plates of those so eager to share in each sugary mouthful. This platform is the pedestal cake plate, an elegant serving piece found in most American homes since its rise in popularity in the 1800s. Often glass or porcelain, cake plates can even be found in wood, Bakelite, and other materials often with an elevated rim to protect the delectables on display from sliding off. Brandy wells or depressions in the center were for holding liquor that provided flavor and ensured moistness of the cake.

During the Depression Era, these pedestal cake plates transitioned into cake plates having less drama, often merely an inch or so higher than the surface of the table. Some cake plates were even flat salvers or serving plates that had no elevation whatsoever. Influencing this lower design is the fact that some cake plates of the 1920s and 1930s were included "free" in packages of flour and simply needed to fit in the sack without displacing too much product.

Serving may include the pleasure of sharing a temptation with others, hence the development of cake carriers in the 1930s. Originally in tin, carriers were produced in copper, chrome, and both aluminum and plastic beginning in the 1950s. Working women of the post-World War II era had little time for frivolous kitchen activities such as baking. Sensitive to this, manufacturers of cake carriers updated the name of their product to "food carriers" providing up to three separate compartments for carrying food to a social event. Cake or food carriers are still being produced in the new millennium, albeit largely in plastic.

There is no end to the size and variety of cake plates and carriers but hundreds of lovely examples are presented in these pages. Pedestal cake plates date to previous centuries and continue through today. Few domestic items that would seem to be unnecessary have stayed in favor for this length of time. The lovely and versatile cake plate reigns supreme in stature, usability, and popularity perhaps because many of us see it as a necessity rather than a luxury.

Contemporary publications often stack two or three pedestal cake plates upon each other creating a dramatic tower of edibles that delight and tempt. However, this presentation is not a recent concept but rather one that has returned to favor. And return it did! For this reason old cake plates are collected and new ones are being manufactured, sadly some as reproductions.

Pictured throughout these pages are utensils for cutting and serving cake. "Cutting the cake: The first requirement for well cut cakes is a thin, pointed, very sharp knife. Serrated (a saw-like edge) or scalloped-edge knives are particularly good for sponge-type cakes. They are excellent for yeast breads, too. Insert the point of the knife into the cake and, keeping the point angled down slightly, saw through the cake with a gentle back and forth motion. Put very little pressure on the knife, let the sharp edge do the work. When you're cutting (multiple pieces) there is always at least one with frosting that sticks to the knife. We dip cake knives in hot water to take the "stick" out of frosting."[4] Throughout the decades the shape and materials for these utensils varied, leaving us with a wonderful array of utilitarian pieces.

Scattered through this book are recipes based on vintage favorites that reflect American taste and sophistication. It is enjoyable to revisit our past, even through the dessert course.

The main focus of this book is on cake plates and carriers made in the late 1920s through the early 1960s one might find in the marketplace. Some patterns of dinnerware never had an actual footed or pedestal cake plate, so in those cases a salver or tray is shown as that is what the woman of the house would have used. Wherever possible, manufacturing information is provided. Values are shown as a guide rather than as firm prices and these values vary immensely according to the condition of the piece, the location of the market, and the overall quality of the design and manufacture. Condition is always of paramount importance in assigning a value. Prices in the Midwest differ from those in the West or East, and those at specialty shows will vary from those at general shows. And, of course, being at the right place at the right time can make all the difference.

Neither the authors nor the publisher is responsible for any outcomes resulting from consulting this book.

[1]*250 Delectable Dessert Recipes* (Chicago, Illinois: Consolidated Book Publishers, 1949).

[2]Justin Bartlett, *Bartlett's Familiar Quotations* (Boston: Little, Brown and Company), 142:29 from George Herbert, "The Size," 1633.

[3]*Our Choicest Recipes – Grace Methodist Episcopal Church, Utica, N.Y.* (Utica, New York: T.J. Griffiths, 1897) p. 23.

[4]*General Foods Kitchens, All About Baking* (New York: Random House, Inc., c. 1960) p. 51.

Chapter One

Early Examples, The Late 1800s

By the late 1800s, Victorian homes provided a huge array of tableware as the style of the day was both elegant and opulent. Some of the most beautiful sterling silver serving utensils were available at this time. Let there be no doubt as to the quantity of pieces available.

LIST OF PIECES

Made in the WILLIAM AND MARY STYLE Flatware

Treasure Solid Silver
REG. U.S. PAT. OFFICE
Sterling 925/1000 Fine

STAPLES

Tea Spoons, Five O'Clock (850)
Tea Spoons, Medium (857)
Tea Spoons, Heavy (*shown actual size*)
Tea Spoons, Extra Heavy
Dessert Spoons, Heavy (*shown actual size*)
Table Spoons, Heavy (868)
Soup Spoons, Heavy (870)
Dessert Forks, Heavy (*shown actual size*)
Dessert Knives, H.H. (*shown actual size*
Dinner Forks, Heavy (854)
Dinner Knives, H.H. (860)
Breakfast Knives, H.H. (855)
Tea Knives

FANCY DOZENS

Berry Forks (858)
Bouillon Spoons (864)
Butter Spreaders, Flat (891)
Butter Spreaders, H.H. (873)
Bread and Butter Knives
Coffee Spoons (865)
Fish Forks, Individual (875)
Five O'Clock Tea Spoons (850)
Fruit Knives, H.H. (890)
Grape Fruit Spoons (*see Orange Spoons*) (886)
Ice Cream Forks (880)
Iced Tea Spoons (878)
Orange Spoons (*also appropriate for Grape Fruit*) (886)
Oyster Forks (869)
Salad Forks, Ind. (875)
Salt Spoons, Ind.

CARVING SETS

Meat, 2 pc., Guards
Meat, 3 pc., Guards
Game, 2 pc., Guards
Game, 3 pc., Guards (861, 862, 863)
Steak, 2 pc., Guards
Steak, 3 pc., Guards
Chop, 2 pc., no Guards

FANCY SINGLE PIECES

Berry Spoon (*see Serving Spoon, Large*) (885)
Bon Bon Spoon
Bon Bon Tongs
Bread Knife, H.H. (872)
Butter Knife (852)
Cake Server, H.H. (889)
Cheese Server, H.H. (883)
Cold Meat Fork (*Serving Fork, Small*) (864)
Cream Ladle (*also appropriate for Salad Dressing and Whipped Cream*) (874)
Cucumber Server (*Flat, Small*) (859)
Duck Shears, H.H. (888)
Egg Server, H.H. (879)
Fish Fork, Serving (*see Serving Fork, Large*) (882)
Fish Knife, Serving (*see Server, Flat, Large*) (892)
Gravy Ladle (877)
Ice Cream Server, H.H. (889)
Ice Cream Server, H.H., W.B. (876) (*Discontinued*)
Jam Spoon
Jelly Server, Tumbler (*also appropriate for Cream Cheese, Honey, etc.*) (866)
Jelly Spoon (*see Serving Spoon, Small*) (887)
Lemon Fork (871)
Mayonnaise Ladle (*see Cream Ladle*) (874)
Olive Fork, Short (856)
Olive Spoon, Short
Pickle Fork, Short (867)
Pie Server, H.H. (889)
Pie Server, H.H., W.B. (876) (*Discontinued*)
Preserve Spoon (*see Serving Spoon, Small*) (887)
Salad Fork, Serving (*see Serving Fork, Large*) (882)
Salad Spoon, Serving (*see Serving Spoon, Large*) (885)
Salt Spoon (881)
Server, Flat, Large (*desirable for Fish, Fried Eggs, Sliced Tomatoes, etc.*) (892)
Server, Flat, Small (*used for Sliced Cucumbers, Croquettes, etc.*) (859)
Serving Fork, Large (*correct service for Salads, appropriate for Serving Fish*) (882)
Serving Fork, Small (*correct fork for Cold Meat. Also used as Small Salad Fork, serving*) (884)
Serving Spoon, Large (*correct service for Salads, Berries, etc.*) (885)
Serving Spoon, Small (*appropriate for serving Preserves, Jelly. Also used as a Small Salad Spoon*) (887)
Sugar Spoon (853)
Sugar Tongs (851)
Tomato Server (*see Server, Flat, Large*) (892)
Waffle Server, H.H. (879)

·16·

Form 518-6-25

A page from *The William and Mary Style* lists staples (bare necessities) and other pieces in solid silver. *Courtesy of Les Fawber & Tom Dibeler / L.E. Fawber Antiques.*

The illustration shows there is little difference in design between cake cutters and pie servers. *Courtesy of Les Fawber & Tom Dibeler / L.E. Fawber Antiques.*

Sterling silver cake/pie server in Ribbon pattern by John R. Wendt, New York, NY; 1870. $225-250. *Courtesy of Les Fawber & Tom Dibeler / L.E. Fawber Antiques.*

Sterling silver utensils and pedestal cake plates created a lovely presentation designed to tempt the guests at one's table. Pedestal cake plates were used to display cakes, tarts, fruits, and more for enjoyment at the conclusion of the meal. Most pedestal cake plates were round, clear glass with pressed designs.

Note the raised rim that prevented the food from sliding off the elevated surface or table. $125. *Courtesy of Susan S. Waters.*

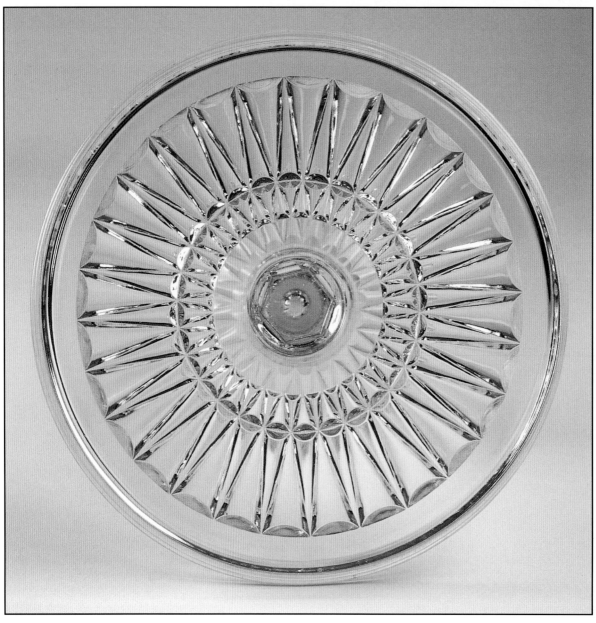

This cake plate does not have a rim, but does feature a skirt or drapery underneath the raised surface that adds drama and elegance. $125. *Courtesy of Susan S. Waters.*

Other designs typical of the late 1800s follow, illustrating common design elements such as skirts, rims, and brandy wells.

$125. Courtesy of Susan S. Waters.

$125. Courtesy of Susan S. Waters.

$125. Courtesy of Susan S. Waters.

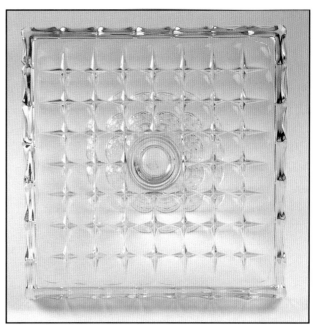

$175. Square shapes are rare and more valuable. This cake plate features drapery and a brandy well. *Courtesy of Susan S. Waters.*

What might Mother prepare for placement upon her lovely pedestal cake plate? From *Our Choicest Recipes – Grace Methodist Episcopal Church*, written in 1897 is a recipe for Angel Food Cake. Typical of its day, it is presented in paragraph form with the ingredients imbedded within the procedure.

Angel Food Cake

Whites of 11 eggs, 1 1/2 cups granulated sugar, 1 cup flour, (measured after being sifted four times), 1 teaspoonful cream of tartar, 1 teaspoonful vanilla or almond, 1/2 teaspoonful salt. Sift the flour and cream of tartar together. Beat the whites of eggs and salt to a stiff froth; that is, until the dish can be turned over without disturbing the contents. Beat the sugar into the eggs, and add the flavoring and flour, stirring quickly and lightly. Bake in a pan with tube in center. Turn upside down on the table after baking, so that a current of air will pass over, and under it. Bake 40 minutes in a moderate oven; do not open the door the first 20 minutes. Do not grease the pan."[1]

[1] *Our Choicest Recipes – Grace Methodist Episcopal Church, Utica, N.Y.* (Utica, New York: T.J. Griffiths, 1897) p. 23.

Chapter Two

The Beginning of the 1900s

The early 1900s was a period of economic growth and prosperity in the United States. The Industrial Revolution led to electricity in most homes, widespread use of indoor plumbing, the introduction of automobiles, and first flight. Ever conscious of detail, the homemaker of the early 1900s served with the elegance and style of the previous century.

Sterling silver cake/pie server in floral repoussé. Unknown manufacturer; circa 1900. $125-175. *Courtesy of Les Fawber & Tom Dibeler / L.E. Fawber Antiques.*

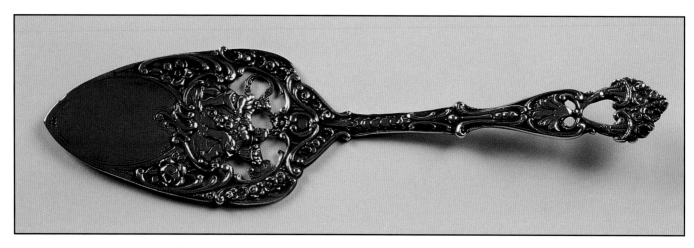

Sterling silver cake/pie server in Continental. Unknown manufacturer; 1900-1920. $80-95. *Courtesy of Les Fawber & Tom Dibeler / L.E. Fawber Antiques.*

Colored glass for general household purposes was becoming more popular in the early 1900s and manufacturers of pedestal cake plates used the opportunity to create lovely wares.

$165. Courtesy of Susan S. Waters.

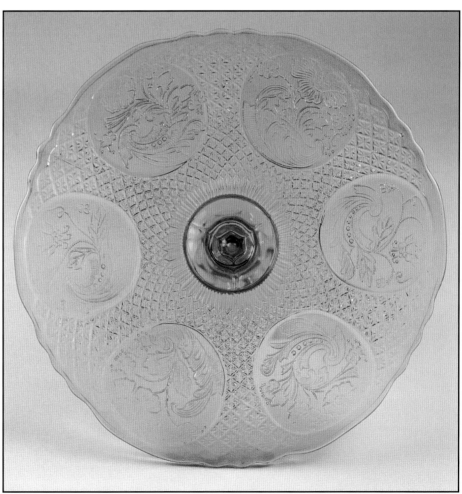

Here's a final look at this sector of Americana prior to the Great Depression. The October 1929 issue of *Better Homes & Gardens* provides insight in a recipe-article entitled, "The Country's Best Cake."

"We know because we have baked them and admired them and eaten them, tasting tidbits carefully and critically for that melting deliciousness and subtle flavor that, after all, distinguish a good cake no matter how pretentious – or unpretentious – the cake may appear." The *Better Homes & Gardens* cake recipe of the year for 1929 was for a Pineapple Cake similar to the following.

Pineapple Cake

1/2 cup butter or margarine
1/2 cup white sugar
4 eggs, separated, use the yolks for the cake
1/2 cup all purpose flour + 2 tablespoons
4 tablespoons milk
1 teaspoon baking powder
pinch of salt

Cream the butter and sugar together, separate the eggs, add only the yolks, well beaten, and mix. Add the 1/2 cup of flour, alternately with the milk. Mix the remaining 2 tablespoons of flour with the baking powder and salt and add last, mixing completely. Pour into two 8-inch round layer cake pans and add the topping that follows.

Pineapple Cake, cont.

Topping

4 egg whites (saved from separating for cake batter)
3/4 cup white sugar
1 1/2 teaspoons vanilla
3/4 cupful of chopped nuts, optional

Beat the egg whites till foamy and then slowly add small amounts of the sugar while continuing to beat. This should be like a meringue and form peaks. Add the vanilla and spread the topping on both unbaked layers. Sprinkle the chopped nuts (if used) and bake for 20 to 25 minutes at 325 to 350 degrees. Allow to cool, then remove from the pans and add the filling that follows.

Pineapple Cake, cont.

Filling

1 cup heavy whipping cream
1-2 tablespoons 10x sugar
1 cup of canned crushed pineapple, drained
1/2 teaspoon vanilla

Place one layer, meringue side down, on a cake plate. Whip the cream, and then add the 10x sugar, drained pineapple, and vanilla while whipping. Spread this mixture on the upside down layer. Lay the other layer on top of this pineapple filling, meringue side up. Serve the same day it is made.

Contemporary serving pieces of this era could have included the following server and pedestal cake plate:

Hollow sterling silver handle with stainless steel blade by the Steiff Company, Boston; circa 1920s. $45-55. *Courtesy of Les Fawber & Tom Dibeler / L.E. Fawber Antiques.*

$85. *Courtesy of Susan S. Waters.*

21

Chapter Three

Depression & Elegant Glass, Named Patterns

The Great Depression began at the end of 1929 and continued into the 1930s. It brought a new entity to the American consumer: glassware free with the purchase of a good or service. Mass-produced with little or no attention to quality, glass companies were able to survive and even prosper during a period of intense economic struggle for most American businesses and citizens. Foods were packaged in glasses with pry-off tops; once the contents were eaten a tumbler was added to the cupboard. Cups and saucers were packaged in soap flakes boxes, and cake plates were placed inside sacks of flour. This phenomenon is now known as Depression Glass. Much of it was free and what was purchased cost mere pennies at best. Early patterns were predominately green with simple motifs molded into the glass. As the acceptance of this glassware increased, a variety of colors and designs followed. During the 1930s pinks, blues, yellows, and greens dominated the spectrum. By the 1940s colored glassware was viewed as old fashioned and clear pieces were most heavily produced.

The dominant focus of this book is cake plates from this era. It is imperative to acknowledge the lack of quality in the production of most of this glassware. Shown are several "Elegant Glass" cake plates manufactured during this period. Depression Glass was free or extremely inexpensive with little concern for quality. By contrast, Elegant Glass was produced by glassmakers known for excellence: Heisey, Paden City, and Duncan & Miller to name a few. Their "elegant" glassware was available in department stores while Depression Glass was found in Woolworth's and other "five and dime" stores.

As cake plates were among the glassware items available free with a purchase, the designs became "flatter" to fit and travel safely in packages. The pedestal was dropped in favor of a ring of glass or three feet or "toes." Some cake plates were made with a small, round foot in the center reminiscent of the pedestal from which it evolved. Other cake plates were salvers, or flat serving plates. Salvers date back to the Victorian era although often thought to be exclusively a Depression era serving plate. Salvers are the largest, round plates made in a given pattern and usually measure from eleven to fourteen inches in diameter. Interesting to note is the fact that many of today's collectors are using salvers as dinner plates finding the eight-to nine-inch dinner plates inadequate.

Space wasn't the only reason that pedestals were abandoned. One must consider the times: poverty was rampant. A lofty pedestal cake plate represented a measure of elegance associated with financial comfort. These were hard times; new times, and a new look mirrored the societal changes. Even serving utensils reflected this evolution from opulent to practical.

Not silver, but silverplate pie/cake server by the Crown Silverplate Company, Bristol, Connecticut; circa 1930s. $10-12. *Courtesy of Les Fawber & Tom Dibeler / L.E. Fawber Antiques.*

Charlotte C. Andersen wrote an article in 1984 entitled, "Depression Recipes Which Aren't Depressing" inspired largely by her mother's practices. Among her mother's insights were several "budget-wise hints" that would apply to cake baking: "Use margarine instead of butter – in her day it has less of Vitamins A and D and she had to color it! But today, fortified with vitamins and colored, it's just as good as butter and much cheaper. Use nonfat dry milk – it's easier to keep than fresh, cheaper, and has all the nutrition, as well as lower fat and cholesterol. If your family won't drink it, you can at least use it in cooking."[1]

Here are the "Baking Rules" put forth in *All About Baking*, a 1936 publication by General Foods:

1. Be orderly.

2. Use good tools.

3. Choose good ingredients.

4. Measure accurately.

5. Mix carefully.

6. Know your pans and oven, and how to cool your cakes.[2]

Extra help in removing a cake from its pan is provided:

Butter cakes-cool on rack about 5 minutes before removing.

Sponge cakes-cool in pan upside down about an hour, or until cold.[3]

The recipes that follow are of particular interest and are based on those from the Depression Era. Start with "Miraculous Cake;" it is the foundation for several cakes that follow. With a few basic ingredients Mother could provide a scrumptious cake in a time when such a treat would have been considered grand indeed!

Miraculous Cake

4 2/3 cups flour
4 1/2 teaspoons baking powder
1 cup shortening
2 cups white sugar
4 eggs, well beaten
1 1/2 cups milk
2 1/2 teaspoons vanilla extract

Completely mix the flour and baking powder, add shortening and sugar gradually. Beat until smooth. Add eggs mixing completely. Slowly add milk, mixing constantly. Finally add vanilla. Divide batter for baking the following cakes.

Prune-Apricot Upside Down Cake

4 tablespoons butter
1/2 cup light brown sugar, firmly packed
13 cooked apricots
6 cooked prunes, halved and pitted
Miraculous Cake batter (recipe above)

Melt butter and sugar in microwave, stir, and pour into 8" square pan. Place apricots and prunes cut-side up on the melted butter and sugar. Alternate an apricot with a prune half. Pour about 1/2 of Miraculous Cake batter over contents of pan. Bake at 350 for 50 minutes, or until done. Loosen cake from sides and bottom of pan with spatula and flip upside down on dish with fruit on top. This is how it is served, hot or cold, garnished with whipped cream.

Spiced Pecan Cakes

2 1/2 tablespoons King Syrup
1/2 teaspoon cloves
1/2 teaspoon nutmeg
1 teaspoon cinnamon

Miraculous Cake batter
1 tablespoon melted butter
2 tablespoons light brown sugar
1/4 cup pecan finely chopped

Grease cup cake or muffin tins. Add syrup and spices to about 1/3 of Miraculous Cake batter and beat well. Pour into cup cake or muffin tins, filling them about 2/3 full. Cover with damp tea towel, then waxed paper, tie securely, and store in refrigerator until cakes are to be baked. Bake in 375 degree oven for 20 minutes, or until almost done. Before removing from oven, mix together melted butter and sugar, and pecans, and sprinkle mixture on top of cakes and bake 2 or 3 minutes longer.

Washington Pie

Miraculous Cake batter
1 cup fruit preserves
10x sugar

Pour about 1/3 of the Miraculous Cake batter into two greased 8" layer pans. Cover closely with damp tea towel, then waxed paper, tie securely, and store in refrigerator until cake is to be baked. Bake in 375 degree oven for 25 minutes or until done. Cool. Spread fruit preserve such as strawberry or apricot or raspberry jam between layers and stack. Decorate by sifting 10x sugar over top of cake.

Pecan Torte

Miraculous Cake batter
2 egg whites
1/2 cup white sugar

1/2 cup coarsely chopped pecans
1/2 cup pecans halves
whipped cream, for garnish

Pour about 1/3 of Miraculous Cake batter into one 8" layer pan. Cover closely with damp tea towel, then waxed paper, tie securely, and store in refrigerator until cake is to be baked. When cake is to be baked, beat egg whites until stiff. Gradually add sugar, 2 tablespoons at a time, beating constantly until sugar is totally mixed and peaks form. Spread mixture on top of Miraculous Cake batter and sprinkle with chopped pecans. Bake at 325 degrees for 25 minutes, then increase to 350 degrees for an additional 30. To serve, garnish with whipped cream and pecans halves.

This brings us to the cake plates on which any of these tempting treats might have been served. The following is an alphabetical arrangement of cake plates by pattern name. More serving pieces and recipes from this era follow at the end of this chapter. We show cake plates individually and also grouped occasionally with additional pieces made in the same pattern.

24

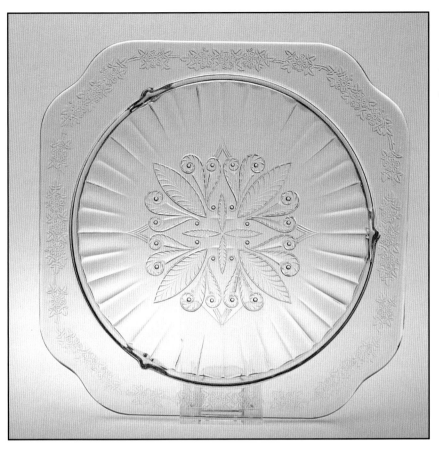

Adam by Jeannette Glass Company, 1932-1934, 10" diameter. $35. Courtesy of Walt & Kim Lemiski – Waltz Time Antiques.

Adam by Jeannette Glass Company, 1932-1934, 10" diameter, shown on far left of back row. $40. Courtesy of Marie Talone.

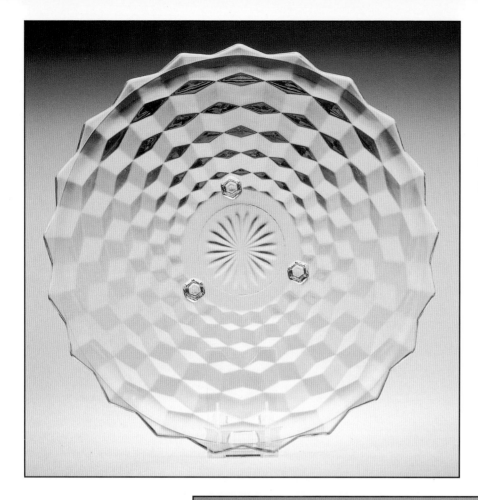

American by Fostoria Glass Company, 1915-1981, 12.5" diameter. $35. *Courtesy of Walt & Kim Lemiski – Waltz Time Antiques.*

American Pioneer by Liberty Works, 1931-1934, 11" diameter. $25. *Courtesy of Bill Quillen.*

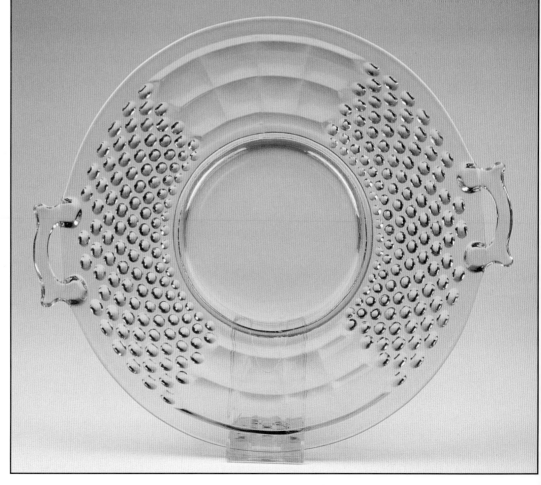

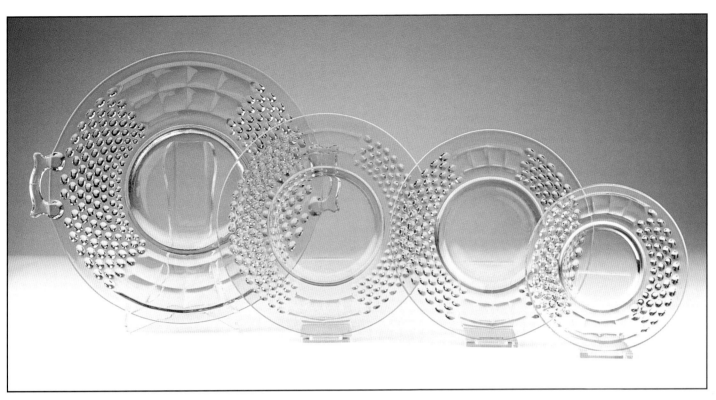

American Pioneer by Liberty Works, 1931-1934, 11" diameter, shown on the far left. $25.
This cake plate was also made in crystal (clear) with a value of $13. *Courtesy of Bill Quillen.*

American Sweetheart by Macbeth-Evans Glass Company, 1930-1936, 12" diameter. $40.
Courtesy of Walt & Kim Lemiski – Waltz Time Antiques.

American Sweetheart by Macbeth-Evans Glass Company, 1930-1936, 15.5" diameter. $500. *Courtesy of Lorraine Penrod.*

American Sweetheart by Macbeth-Evans Glass Company, 1930-1936, 12" diameter. $35. *Courtesy of Walt & Kim Lemiski – Waltz Time Antiques.*

American Sweetheart by Macbeth-Evans Glass Company, 1930-1936. Either of the two large plates could be utilized as they have diameters of 12" and 15.5". Larger, $425; smaller, $220. Courtesy of Lorraine Penrod.

Avocado by Indiana Glass Company, 1923-1933, 12.5" x 10.5" shown in back. $55. Courtesy of Ted Bradley.

Avocado by Indiana Glass Company, 1923-
1933, 12.5" x 10.5" shown on the far left of
the back row. $75. Courtesy of Ted Bradley.

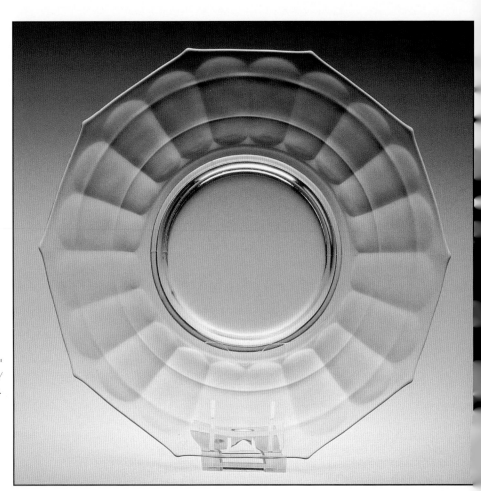

Bamboo Optic by Liberty Works, 1929, 10.75"
diameter. $35. Courtesy of Norma Peacock/
Peacock Antiques.

Block Optic by Hocking Glass Company, 1929-1933, 10.25" diameter. $30. A larger plate with a 12.75" diameter is available only in green and yellow in this pattern with a value of $35 for green and $30 for yellow. *Courtesy of Wayne & Jean Boyd.*

Block Optic by Hocking Glass Company, 1929-1933, 10.25" diameter shown on the left. $30.

Cameo by Hocking Glass Company, 1930-1934, 10" diameter with three feet.
$45 in green. The 10.5" rimmed plate also acts as a cake plate with a value of
$125 in green and $250 in pink. *Courtesy of David G. Baker.*

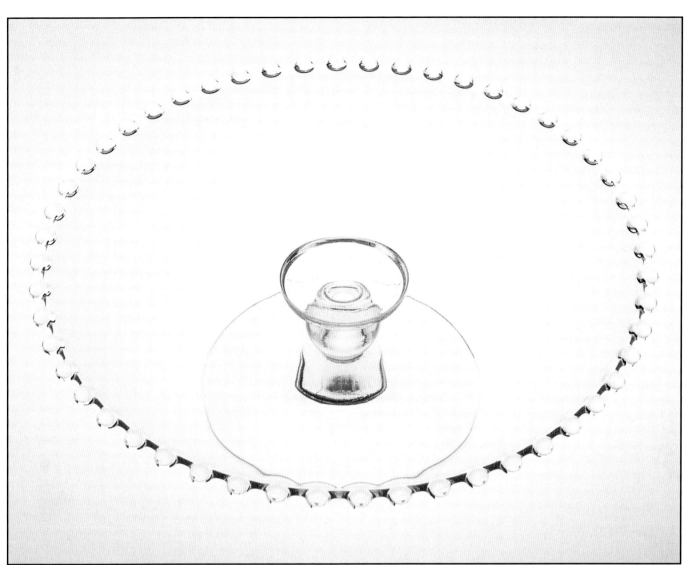

Candlewick by Imperial Glass Company, 1936-1982, 10" diameter. $100. Courtesy of Aimée Schuld.

Candlewick
by Imperial
Glass
Company,
1936-1982,
10" diameter
with 3"
pedestal.
$150.
*Courtesy of
Aimée Schuld.*

Caprice by Cambridge, 1936-1957, 11.25" diameter with three feet. $100. Courtesy of Walt & Kim Lemiski – Waltz Time Antiques.

Caprice by Cambridge, 1936-1957, 11.25" diameter with three feet and silver overlay. $40. Courtesy of Walt & Kim Lemiski – Waltz Time Antiques.

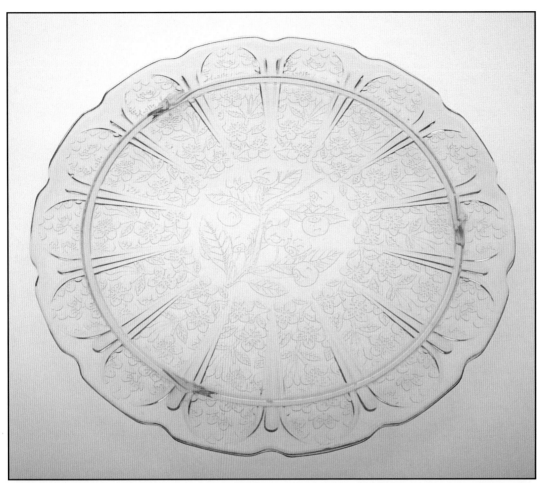

Cherry Blossom by Jeannette Glass Company, 1930-1939, 10.25" diameter. $45 in green and $35 in pink. *Courtesy of Walt & Kim Lemiski – Waltz Time Antiques.*

Cherry Blossom by Jeannette Glass Company, 1930-1939. The 10.5" diameter tray shown in the back row on the right is the only option in Delphite. $35. *Courtesy of Bob & Cindy Bentley.*

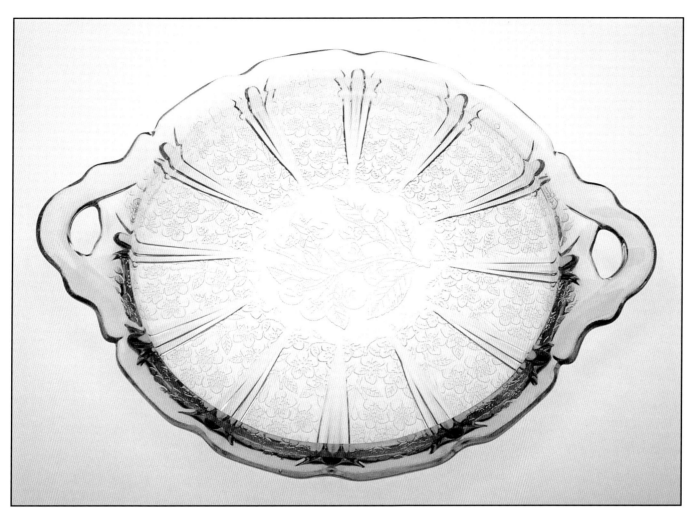

Cherry Blossom by Jeannette
Glass Company, 1930-1939,
10.5" diameter. $45. *Courtesy
of Walt & Kim Lemiski – Waltz
Time Antiques.*

Chinex Classic with castle motif
by Macbeth-Evans Division of
Corning Glass Works, late
1930s-1942, 11.5" diameter.
$25.

Chinex Classic with tomato motif by Macbeth-Evans Division of Corning Glass Works, late 1930s-1942, 12" diameter. $30.

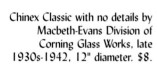

Chinex Classic with no details by Macbeth-Evans Division of Corning Glass Works, late 1930s-1942, 12" diameter. $8.

Christmas Candy by Indiana Glass Company, late 1930s-early 1950s. The 11.25" plate shown in the center of the back row is the only plate available in this pattern. *Courtesy of Wes & Carla Davidson.*

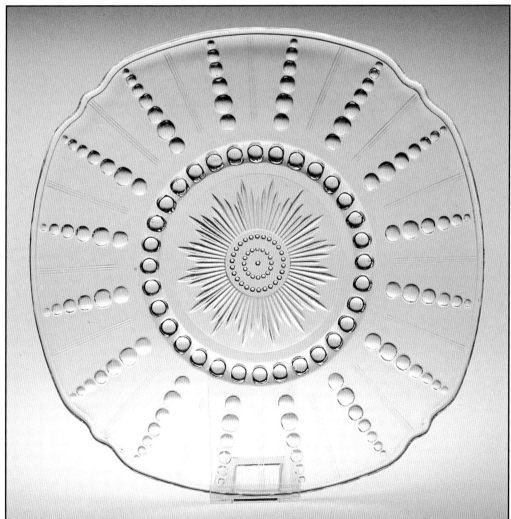

Columbia by Federal Glass Company, 1938-1942, 11" diameter. $15. *Courtesy of Walt & Kim Lemiski – Waltz Time Antiques.*

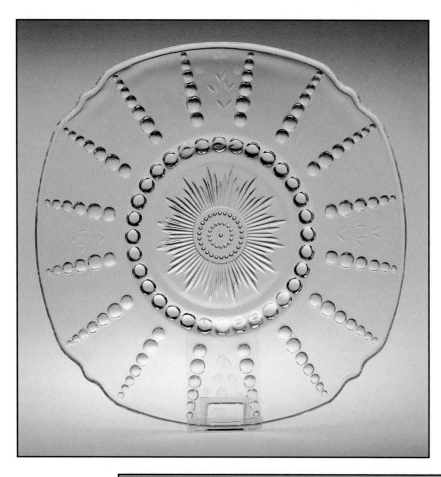

Columbia by Federal Glass Company, 1938-1942, 11" diameter with Canadian cuts, possibly done to avoid certain importing fees. $15. *Courtesy of Walt & Kim Lemiski – Waltz Time Antiques.*

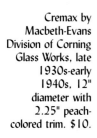

Cremax by Macbeth-Evans Division of Corning Glass Works, late 1930s-early 1940s, 12" diameter with 2.25" peach-colored trim. $10.

Cremax by
Macbeth-Evans
Division of
Corning Glass
Works, late
1930s-early
1940s, 12"
diameter with 2"
yellow trim. $10.

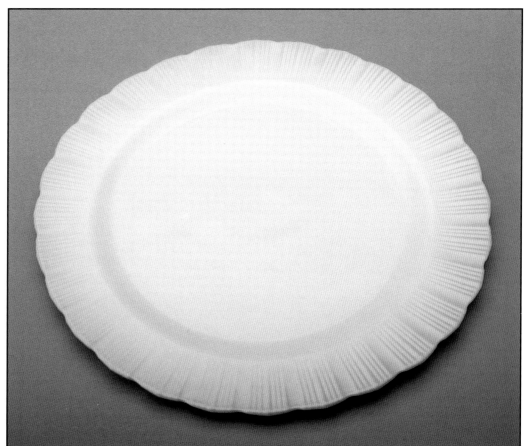

Cremax by Macbeth-Evans Division
of Corning Glass Works, late
1930s-early 1940s, 12" diameter
with 2" green trim. $10.

41

Cremax by Macbeth-Evans Division of Corning Glass Works, late 1930s-early 1940s, 12" diameter with floral design. $10.

Cremax by Macbeth-Evans Division of Corning Glass Works, late 1930s-early 1940s, 12" diameter with floral design. $10.

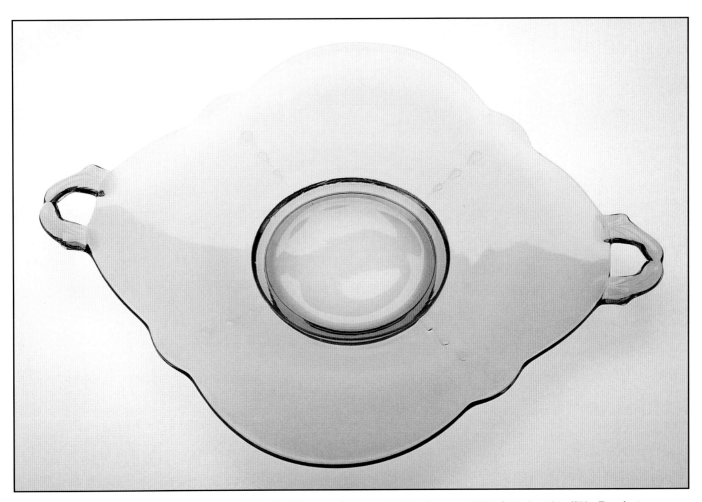

Crow's Foot by Paden City Glass Company, 1930s, 11.75" across the diagonal. $40. Courtesy of Walt & Kim Lemiski – Waltz Time Antiques.

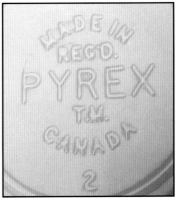

Crown by Pyrex, Macbeth-Evans Division of Corning Glass Works, 1940s, 12" diameter. $27. Courtesy of Walt & Kim Lemiski – Waltz Time Antiques.

43

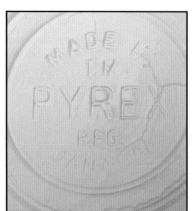

Crystal Crest by Fenton Art Glass Company, early 1940s. 12.25" diameter with 1.5" pedestal. $50.

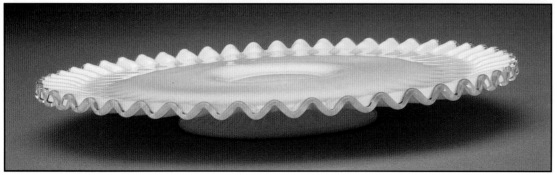

Cupid by Paden City Glass Company, 1930s, 11.25" diameter, 1.75" tall foot, on left. $225. Courtesy of Neil McCurdy – Hoosier Kubboard Glass.

Detail of pattern.

Cupid by Paden City Glass Company, 1930s, 11.25" diameter, 1.75" tall foot in back showing
the table or surface where a cake would be placed. $225. *Courtesy of Doris McMullen.*

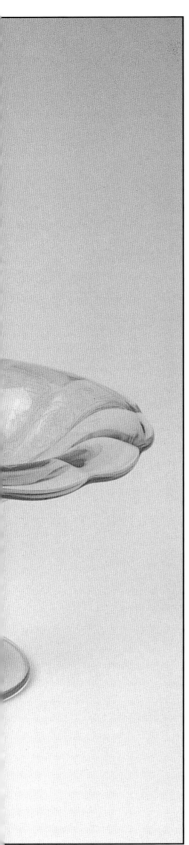

Daisy by Indiana Glass Company, amber in 1940, 11.5" diameter. $18. Crystal was made in 1933 with a value of $7.

Della Robbia by Westmoreland Glass Company, 1928-1940s, 14" diameter. $80 with foot, $50 without foot as shown. *Courtesy of Walt & Kim Lemiski – Waltz Time Antiques.*

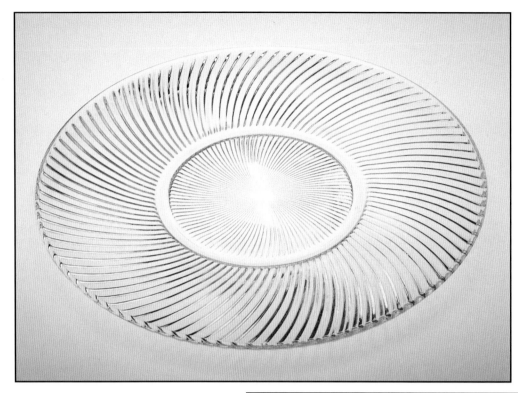

Diana by Federal Glass Company,
1937-1941, 11.5" diameter.
$10.

Diana by Federal Glass Company, 1937-1941,
11.5" diameter. Shown with gold trim, $12.
Courtesy of Norma Peacock/Peacock Antiques.

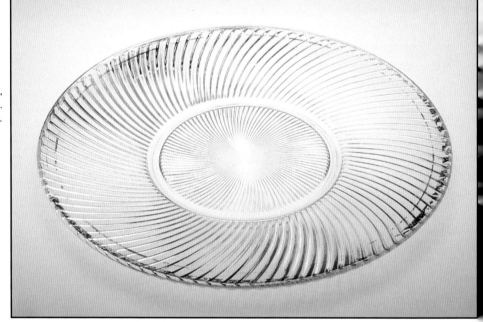

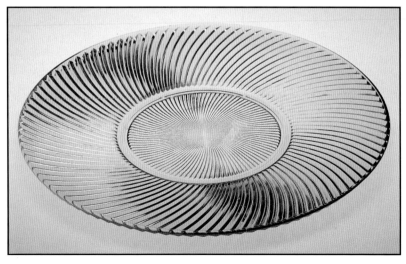

Diana by Federal Glass Company, 1937-
1941, 11.5" diameter. $20. *Courtesy of
Michael Rothenberger / Mike's Collectibles.*

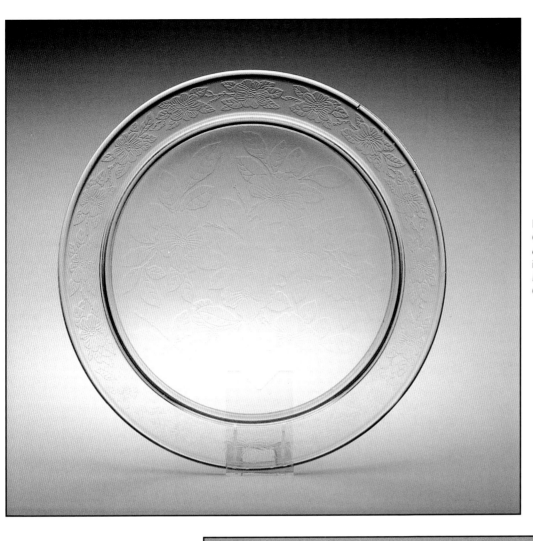

Dogwood by Macbeth-Evans Glass Company, 1930-1934, 13" diameter with solid ring. $150. This is also found in green, $150; and Monax, $200. *Courtesy of David G. Baker.*

Dogwood by Macbeth-Evans Glass Company, 1930-1934, 11.5" diameter. $20; found in pink, $45. *Courtesy of Marie Talone.*

Doric by Jeannette Glass Company,
1935-1938, 10.25" diameter. $30.
Courtesy of Norma Peacock/Peacock
Antiques.

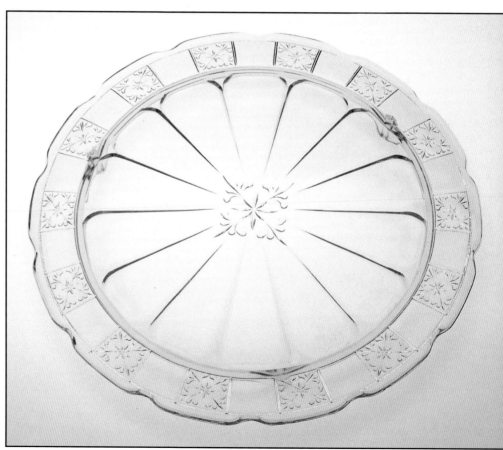

Doric by Jeannette Glass Company,
1935-1938, 10.25" diameter
shown in the middle of the back row.
$40. Courtesy of Charlie
Diefenderfer.

Hobnail (Number 118 Pattern) by
Duncan & Miller Glass Company,
1930-1940s, 11.5" diameter with
two handles. $45.

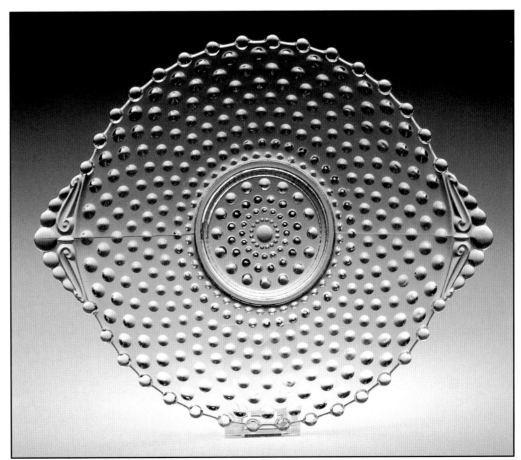

Iris by Jeannette Glass Company, 1928-1932, 12" diameter. $50. *Courtesy of Walt & Kim Lemiski – Waltz Time Antiques.*

Jubilee by Lancaster Glass Company, 1930, 11" diameter shown in the middle. $50. *Courtesy of Barbara L. Jaquett.*

Landrum by Lancaster Glass Company, 1932, 11" diameter. $40.

Lincoln Inn by Fenton Art Glass Company, 1928-1929, 11.5" diameter. This pattern was produced in a vast array of colors and the cake plate is worth $50 regardless of color. *Courtesy of Neil McCurdy – Hoosier Kubboard Glass.*

Lincoln Inn by Fenton Art Glass Company, 1928-1929, 11.5" diameter, the large plate in the center of the grouping. Crystal (clear) can be found with a fruit motif in the center and will be 30% more than the $50 value for the plain plate. *Courtesy of Kathy McCarney.*

Madrid by Federal Glass Company, 1932-1938, 12" diameter. $40. *Courtesy of David G. Baker.*

Madrid by Federal Glass Company, 1932-1938, 12" diameter. $30. Courtesy of Michael Rothenberger / Mike's Collectibles.

Manhattan by Anchor Hocking Glass Company, 1939-1941, 14" diameter. $35. Courtesy of Michael Rothenberger / Mike's Collectibles.

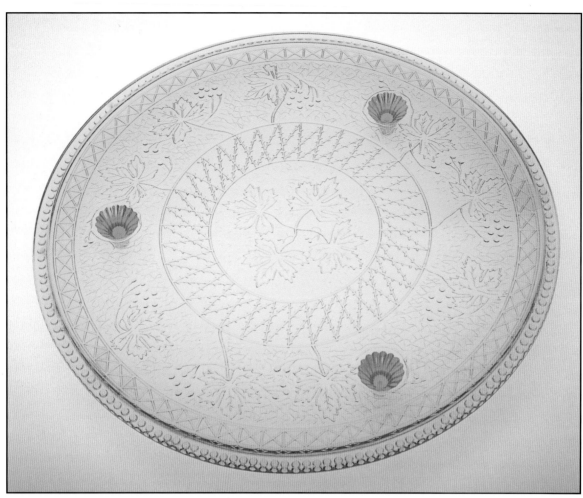

Maple Leaf thought to be by United States Glass Company, circa early 1930s, 12.25" diameter. $40.

Maya by Paden City Glass Manufacturing Company, 11.75" diameter with center foot and silver overlay. $75. *Courtesy of Walt & Kim Lemiski – Waltz Time Antiques.*

Mayfair by Hocking Glass Company, 1931-1936, 12" diameter. Satinized pink, $70. Courtesy of Norma Peacock/Peacock Antiques.

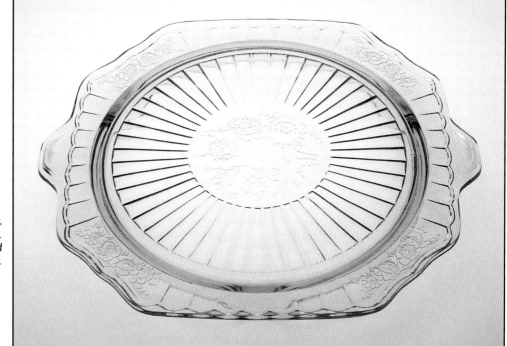

Mayfair by Hocking Glass Company, 1931-1936, 10" diameter. $70. Courtesy of Janice Johnston / Behind The Green Door.

Mayfair by Hocking
Glass Company,
1931-1936, 10"
diameter, in back
row on left. $100
in blue and green.
Courtesy of Paul
Reichwein.

Miss America by
Hocking Glass
Company, 1933-
1936, 12"
diameter. $90.
Courtesy of Wayne
& Jean Boyd.

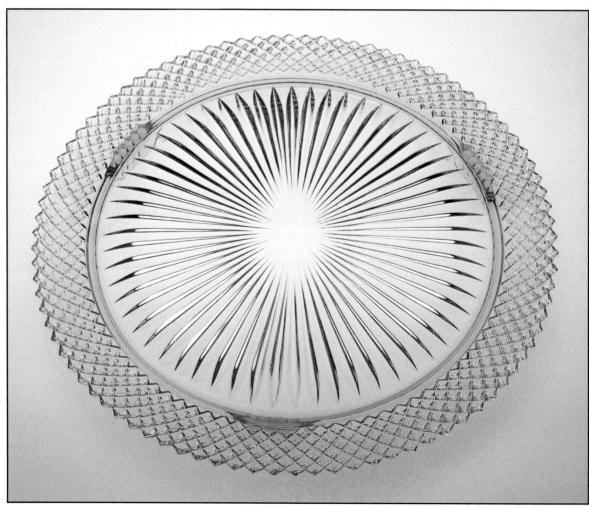

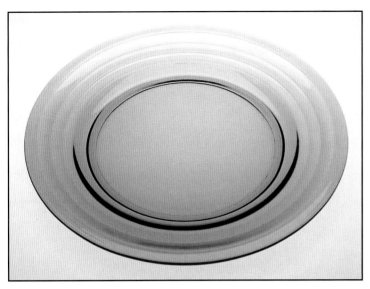

Moderntone by Hazel-Atlas Glass Company, 1930s, 10.5" diameter. $100 in cobalt, $65 in amethyst. *Courtesy of David G. Baker.*

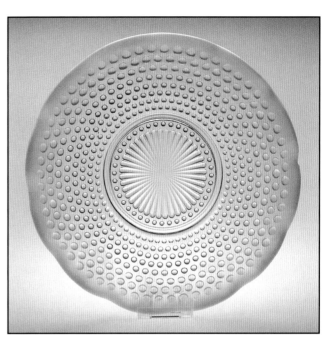

Moonstone by Hocking Glass Company, 1942-1946, 11" diameter. $38. *Courtesy of Walt & Kim Lemiski – Waltz Time Antiques.*

Moondrops by New Martinsville Glass Manufacturing Company, 1932-1940s. This 13.5" plate was made in red and cobalt, $70, and as shown, ice blue, $40. *Courtesy of Carl L. Pellham.*

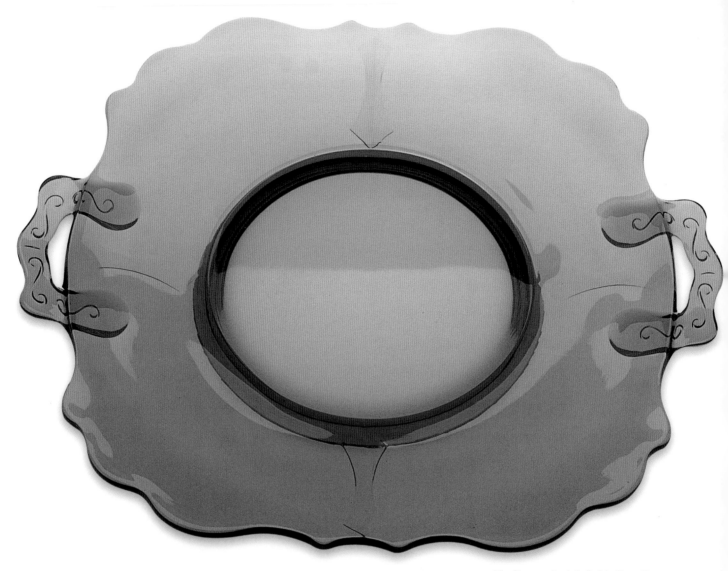

Mt. Pleasant by L.E. Smith Glass Company,
1930s, 10" diameter. $35.

Mt. Pleasant by L.E. Smith Glass Company, 1930s,
10" diameter. $35. *Courtesy of Norma Peacock/
Peacock Antiques.*

Newport by Hazel-Atlas Glass Company, mid-
1930s, 11.5" diameter. $55 in amethyst or
cobalt. *Courtesy of David. G. Baker.*

Oxford by Corning Glass Works,
Macbeth-Evans Division, 1940-1941,
12" diameter. $12.

Oyster and Pearl by Anchor Hocking
Glass Company, 1938-1940, 13"
diameter. $35. *Courtesy of Norma
Peacock/Peacock Antiques.*

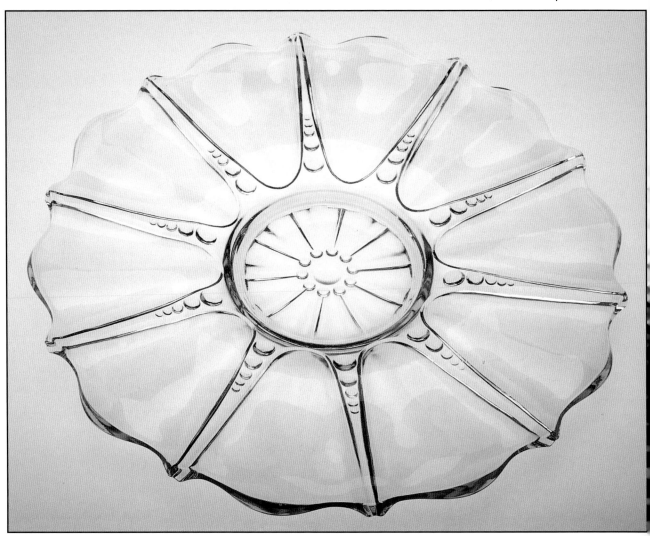

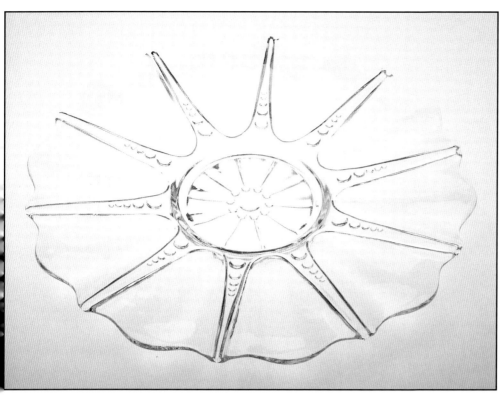

Oyster and Pearl by Anchor Hocking Glass Company, 1938-1940, 13" diameter. $12 as shown in crystal (clear) and $60 in ruby. *Courtesy of David G. Baker.*

Patrick by Lancaster Glass Company, 1930s, 11" diameter. $140 in yellow and $175 in pink. *Courtesy of Michael Rothenberger / Mike's Collectibles.*

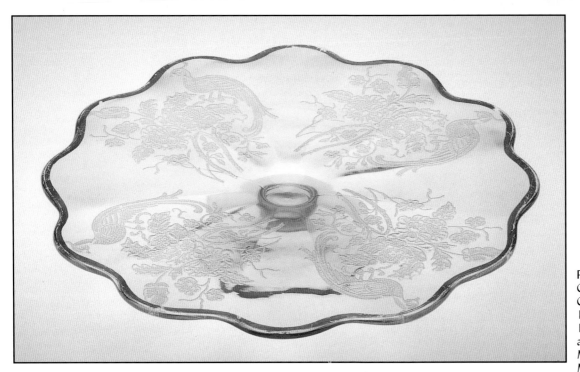

Peacock and Rose by Paden City Glass Manufacturing Company, 1928-1930s, 11.25" diameter with 1.75" pedestal. $150 in any color. *Courtesy of Michael Rothenberger / Mike's Collectibles.*

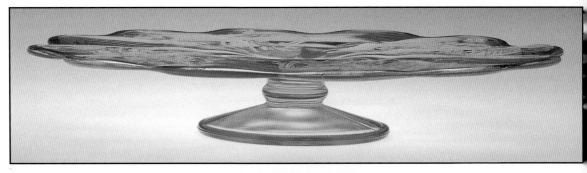

Petalware by Macbeth-Evans Glass Company, 1930-1940, 10.75" diameter. $15. *Courtesy of Wayne and Jean Boyd.*

Petalware by Macbeth-Evans Glass Company, 1930-1940, 10.75" diameter. $25. *Courtesy of Walt & Kim Lemiski – Waltz Time Antiques.*

Petalware by Macbeth-Evans Glass Company, 1930-1940, 10.75" diameter. $40. *Courtesy of Marie Talone.*

Philbe by Hocking Glass Company, 1940, 11.5" diameter. $300 in blue, $125 in pink and green, $50 in crystal (clear).

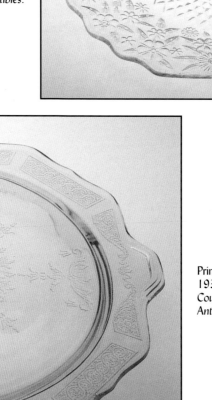

Pineapple and Floral by Indiana Glass Company, 1932-1937, 11.5" diameter. $10 in any color. *Courtesy of Michael Rothenberger / Mike's Collectibles.*

Princess by Hocking Glass Company, 1931-1934, 10" diameter. $50 in green or pink. *Courtesy of Walt & Kim Lemiski – Waltz Time Antiques.*

Queen Mary by Hocking Glass Company, 1936-1939, 14" diameter. $25. Add $8 for the chrome cover.

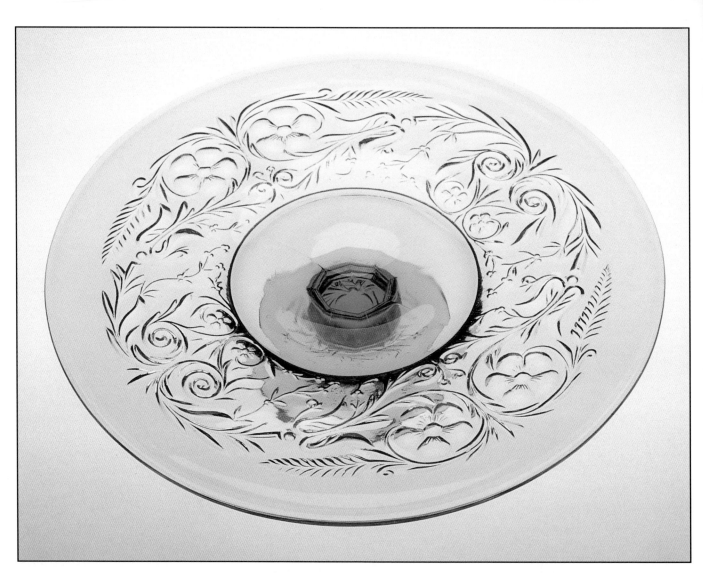

Rock Crystal Flower by McKee Glass Company, 1922-1931, 11" diameter
with 2.5" pedestal. $125 in red, $100 in cobalt, $40 in crystal (clear), $60
in all other colors. *Courtesy of Wayne and Jean Boyd.*

Romanesque by L.E. Smith Glass Company, late 1920s, 11.25" diameter with 3" pedestal. $80 in any color. *Courtesy of Dave and Jamie Moriarty.*

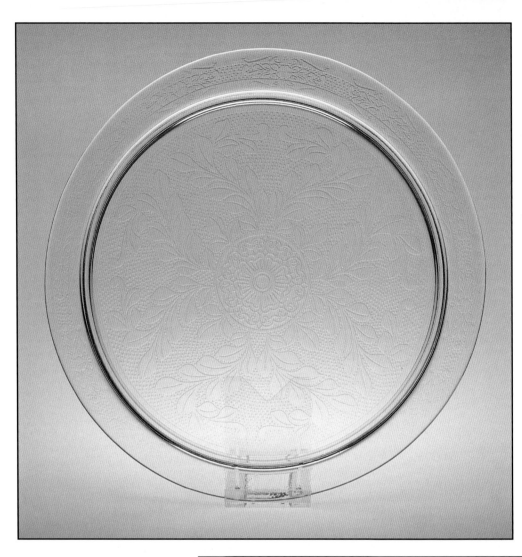

"S" pattern by Macbeth-Evans Glass Company, 1930-1932, 11.5" diameter. $60 in topaz, $30 in crystal (clear) with trim, $20 as shown. *Courtesy of Norma Peacock/Peacock Antiques.*

Sandwich by Indiana Glass Company, 1920s-1980s, 13" diameter with solid ring. $30.

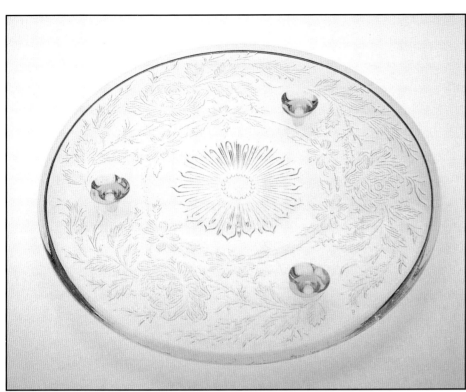

Shaggy Rose by United States Glass Company, 1930, 10" diameter. $45. Courtesy of Walt & Kim Lemiski – Waltz Time Antiques.

Sharon by Federal Glass Company, 1935-1939, 11.5" diameter. $10. Courtesy of Norma Peacock/Peacock Antiques.

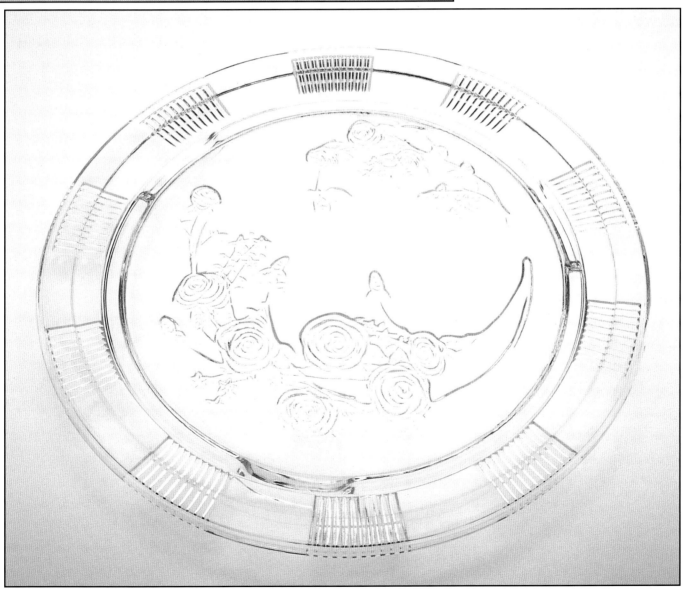

Sharon by Federal Glass Company, 1935-1939, 11.5" diameter. $20 in amber, $70 in green. *Courtesy of David G. Baker.*

Sharon by Federal Glass Company, 1935-1939, 11.5" diameter. $50. *Courtesy of Sylvia A. Brown.*

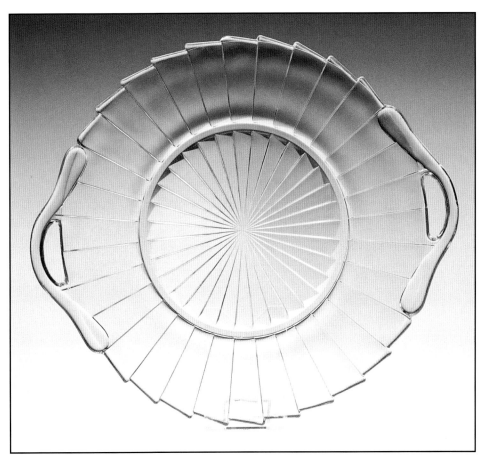

Sierra by Jeannette Glass Company, 1930-1933, 10" diameter. $25. Courtesy of Walt & Kim Lemiski – Waltz Time Antiques.

Sierra by Jeannette Glass Company, 1930-1933, 10" diameter. $25. Courtesy of Marie Talone.

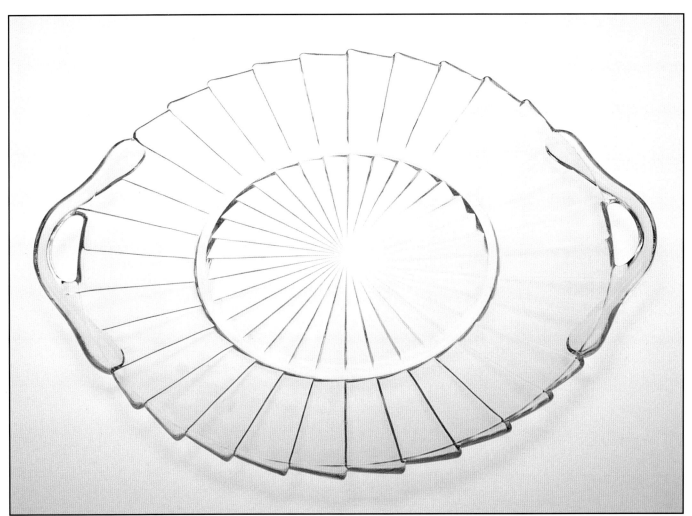

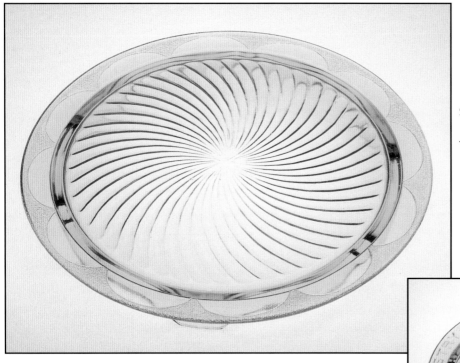

Spiral by Hocking Glass Company, 1928-1930, 10" diameter. $30. Courtesy of Julie and Jim Retzloff.

Spiral by Hocking Glass Company, circa 1929, 10" diameter with advertisement. $150. Courtesy of Walt & Kim Lemiski – Waltz Time Antiques.

Spiral Optic by Tiffin, circa 1930s, 10" diameter. $75. Courtesy of Julie and Jim Retzloff.

Starlight by Hazel-Atlas Glass Company, 1938, 13" diameter. $25 in pink, $18 in clear (crystal). Shown doubling as an under plate for a 12" bowl. Courtesy of Marie Talone.

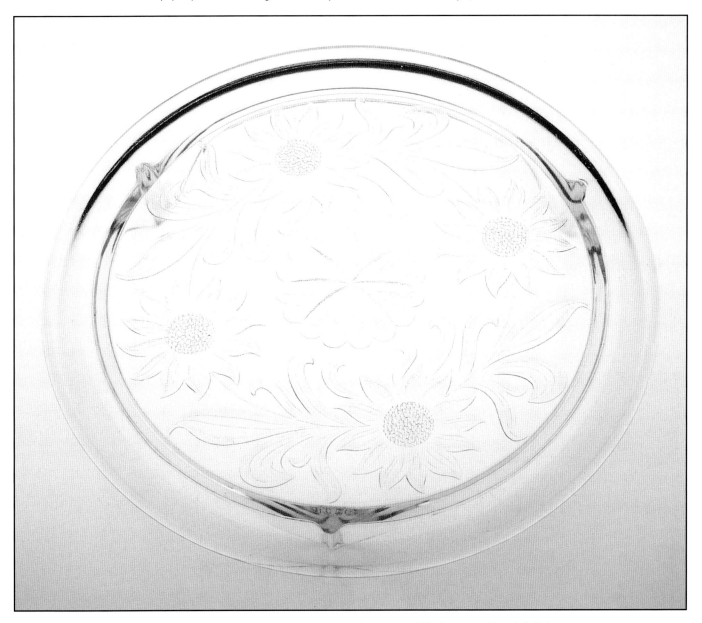

Sunflower by Jeannette Glass Company, 1930s, 10" diameter. $30. Courtesy of David G. Baker.

Sunflower by Jeannette Glass Company, 1930s, 10" diameter. $25 in light green as shown and dark green. *Courtesy of Norma Peacock/Peacock Antiques.*

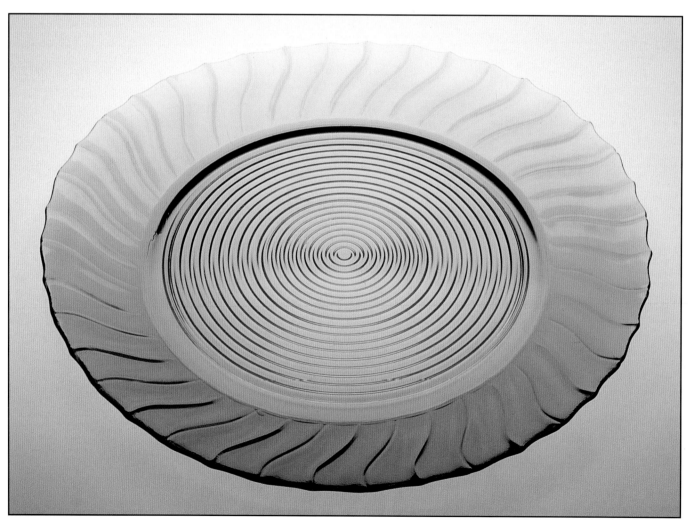

Swirl by Jeannette Glass Company, 1937-1938, 13.25" diameter. $35. *Courtesy of Walt & Kim Lemiski – Waltz Time Antiques.*

Swirl by Jeannette Glass Company, 1937-1938, 12.75" diameter. $25.

Thistle by Macbeth-Evans Glass Company, 1929-1930, 13" diameter with solid ring. $175 in green, $150 in pink. *Courtesy of Diefenderfer's Collectibles & Antiques.*

Tulip by Dell Glass Company, 1930s, 10.5" plate. Tulip colors are featured in this grouping. Amethyst and blue, $45; green and amber, $35; crystal (clear), $20.

Twisted Optic by Imperial Glass Company, 1927-1930, 12" diameter shown on the right in the back row. $25. *Courtesy of Julie and Jim Retzloff.*

Vernon by Indiana Glass Company, 1931, 11" diameter. $35 in green and yellow, $12 in crystal (clear).

Waterford by Hocking Glass Company, 1938-1944, 10.25" diameter. $35 in pink, $15 in crystal (clear). *Courtesy of Janice Johnston / Behind The Green Door.*

Wheat by unknown, c. 1930s, 12.25" diameter. $45.

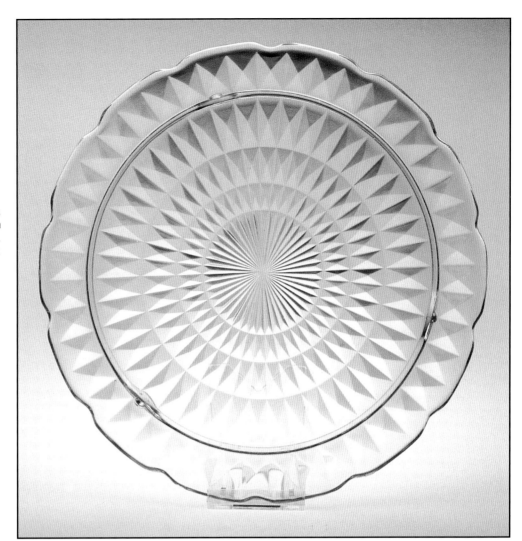

Windsor by Jeannette Glass Company, 1932-1946, 10.25" diameter. $35 in green and pink, $10 in crystal (clear). Courtesy of David G. Baker.

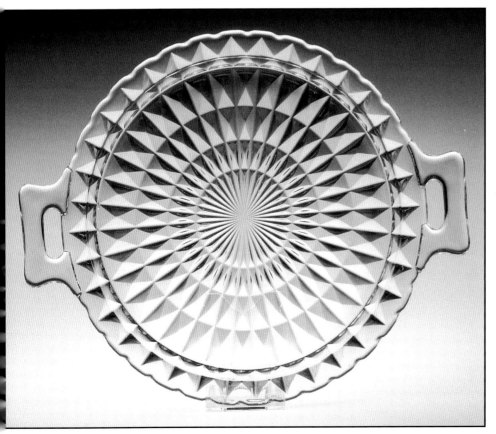

Windsor by Jeannette Glass Company, 1932-1946, 10.25" diameter. $20 in green and pink, $8 in crystal (clear). Courtesy of Walt & Kim Lemiski – Waltz Time Antiques.

Serving Utensils — Bakelite and More

Invented at the turn of the twentieth century and developed as a material to insulate electricity, Bakelite was introduced to the American homemaker in the form of knives in the middle of the 1920s. Quite expensive at several dollars apiece, household use of Bakelite was delayed until the economic recovery of the mid-1930s. Although Bakelite kitchenware was made into the 1950s, it was primarily at its peak in use and popularity from the middle of the 1930s and through the 1940s.

Presented are a variety of Bakelite-handled utensils from this period. Sometimes free with the purchase of a product, our mothers and grandmothers would probably be appalled at the values they now have. All work extremely well but do require hand washing.

Shown below are four variations on a theme: each server has a slightly different semi-triangular blade and unique handle treatment. Only the second and fourth servers are marked "Germany" but based on similarities of design one can assume all are German in origin. Each is very much in demand as collectors particularly like handles with multiple colors whether in divided sections or swirled together in an "end-of-the-day" handle as shown on the right. "End-of-the-day" handles are so named because factory workers mixed colors together at the end of the workday creating unique and colorful handles.

$40 each.

All three servers on the right are in high demand. On top is the 10" long Androck "bullet" handle, a favorite with today's collectors. The 1934 patented design in the middle is extremely rare. It features two .75" spikes that prick the side of a piece of cake when the blade is slid underneath a slice to be lifted. The spikes assist in steadying the portion being served allowing the hostess to appear in total control as theoretically her fingers never need to touch someone's dessert. Another 10" Androck "bullet" is at the bottom featuring a curved blade patented in 1936.

Designs can be simple as illustrated below on the 9.5" pie or cake server made with a stainless steel triangular blade inserted into a Bakelite handle. However, this was a period of time with many factories in competition for the consumer dollar and uniqueness mattered. Patents from 1870 and 1873 are the only marks on an extremely clever and exceedingly rare 9.25" server made with a blade that is bent on a ninety-degree angle.

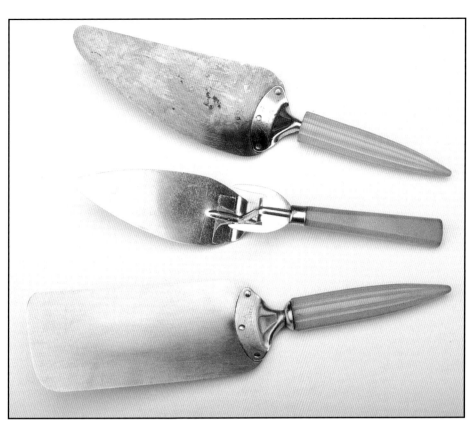

Top, $24; middle, $35; bottom, $24.

Top, bent blade, $45; bottom, $15.

The design of a cake breaker is so efficient that other than handle treatment it remained unchanged for decades. Although Bakelite was considered old-fashioned by the 1950s, cake breakers like the ones shown were produced well into the 1950s and were among the final Bakelite kitchen items manufactured.

Red Bakelite cake breakers are abundant and one must wonder if they might have been a premium received free with a purchase of some kind; when purchased, they were less than a dollar. Today red is the lowest in value as there is an abundant supply. There are subtle handle differences that make some more valuable than others but overall red is one's best buy if color isn't an issue.

All three of these cake breakers shown above right have identical handles. The difference in values is a direct result of supply (how many are available today) and demand (which ones collectors seek). These are 10.5" in length with handles that are just over 3.5".

Because of the rare color and extreme amount of marbling (swirling of color), the

Yellow, $18; red, $10; black, $15.

green Bakelite cake breaker shown below has a higher value than the ones shown in the previous picture. The red cake breaker is actually Lucite, which is easy to determine because it is transparent. The round-handled cake breaker is an "end-of-the-day" Bakelite handle: colors were mixed together at the end of the workday and factory workers created what

contemporary collectors consider to be among the most alluring and desirable Bakelite examples. Some of the most unique Bakelite designs come from Canada as is true for the 12" long golf club cake breaker. Probably a novelty item for golf fanatics, it is extremely rare as well as amusing.

Green, $20; red, $20; end-of-the-day, $45; golf club, $35.

Don't forget the icing! Androck produced a huge variety of "bullet" handled kitchen tools. Shown are two spreaders with stainless steel blades.

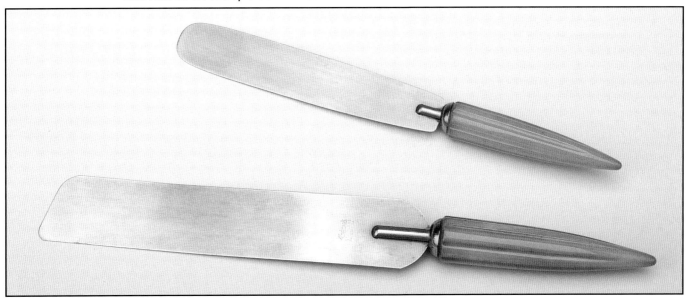

8.5" long, $25; 11" long, $20.

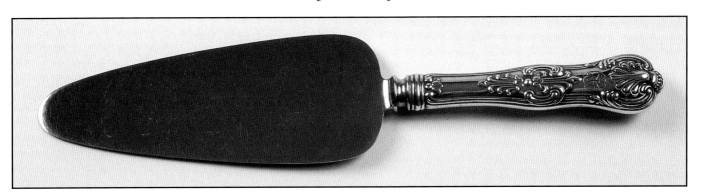

Sterling silver handle with stainless steel blade cake server. Unknown manufacturer, circa 1940s. $35-40. *Courtesy of Les Fawber & Tom Dibeler / L.E. Fawber Antiques.*

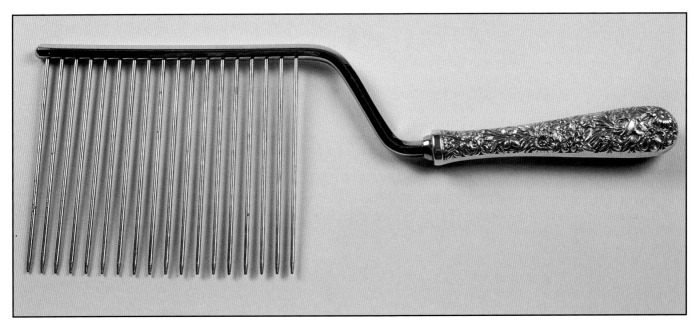

This is a more formal cake breaker with a hollow sterling silver handle and a stainless steel blade by S. Kirk & Son, Baltimore, circa 1940s. $45-65. *Courtesy of Les Fawber & Tom Dibeler / L.E. Fawber Antiques.*

Here's a great recipe! When Barbara was first introduced to *Tomato Soup Cake* she thought it was a novel recipe way, way back in the 1970s. Finding it labeled a "classic" in the 1940s was a huge surprise. It's time to revisit this 1940s classic.

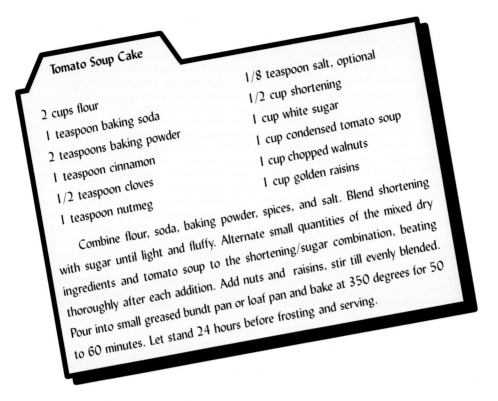

Tomato Soup Cake

2 cups flour
1 teaspoon baking soda
2 teaspoons baking powder
1 teaspoon cinnamon
1/2 teaspoon cloves
1 teaspoon nutmeg

1/8 teaspoon salt, optional
1/2 cup shortening
1 cup white sugar
1 cup condensed tomato soup
1 cup chopped walnuts
1 cup golden raisins

Combine flour, soda, baking powder, spices, and salt. Blend shortening with sugar until light and fluffy. Alternate small quantities of the mixed dry ingredients and tomato soup to the shortening/sugar combination, beating thoroughly after each addition. Add nuts and raisins, stir till evenly blended. Pour into small greased bundt pan or loaf pan and bake at 350 degrees for 50 to 60 minutes. Let stand 24 hours before frosting and serving.

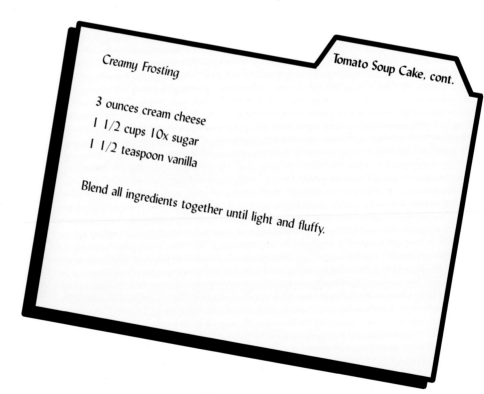

Creamy Frosting

Tomato Soup Cake, cont.

3 ounces cream cheese
1 1/2 cups 10x sugar
1 1/2 teaspoon vanilla

Blend all ingredients together until light and fluffy.

[1]Charlotte C. Andersen, "Depression Recipes Which Aren't Depressing," *Women's Circle Home Cooking*, (House of White Birches, Inc./Tower Press) May, 1984.
    [2]*All About Home Baking*, General Foods Corporation (New York, 1936), pp. 8-9.
    [3]Ibid, p. 27.

Chapter Four

Depression & Elegant Glass, Canadian Corn Flower

What is Corn Flower? The following background was written by Canadian Glass expert Walt Lemiski, M.A.

The founder of the W.J. Hughes Corn Flower Company, William John Hughes, was born in Dufferin County, Ontario, Canada in the early 1880s. As a young man he was employed by Roden Brothers silversmiths of Toronto. Fortunately for him and for glass collectors, when that firm expanded their lines to include cut lead glass Hughes was asked to learn the art of cutting. Starting in 1912, he began to experiment at his home with his own original "grey" cut glass patterns (shallower cuts on lighter glass). In 1914, Hughes left Roden Brothers to devote himself full time to producing and selling Corn Flower glass. The Hughes Corn Flower pattern is distinctive with its 12 petalled flower, grid-like interior, and elegant sweeping stems.

Through the first several decades of Hughes Corn Flower production, the blanks ordered by the company came from the tri-state area of Pennsylvania, Ohio, and West Virginia. These three states were home to all the major American glass producers and accounted for over ninety percent of glass production in North America throughout this period. Essential for the Corn Flower decoration that Hughes cut was fine quality glassware. What one thinks of as typical Depression Glass is scarcely better than bottle glass. Inherent in such low-grade glass were bubbles, lack of clarity and non-uniformity of shape. What Corn Flower was primarily cut upon was Elegant Glass, also known as "hand glass." This was made in considerably smaller batches with superior materials. Hughes looked for quality glassware and for blanks that were uncluttered in design leaving large clear surfaces on which to better showcase his original Corn Flower design. Most of the companies that supplied glass to Hughes were major players in the American elegant glass field: Central, Duncan and Miller, Fostoria, Heisey, Imperial, Jeannette, Lancaster, New Martinsville, Paden City, Tiffin, and West Virginia Specialty glass companies.

Although Corn Flower glass was produced for seventy-five years, the most sought after items these days are the pre-1950 items. First among these are the colored items followed by the crystal (clear) items with excellent cuts. One can recognize the earlier items by their fuller cutting, larger flowers, and tendency towards a wreathing effect with the leaves surrounding the floral pattern. Many of these earlier blanks also have beading – a series of cuts, like a pie-crust, found at the edges, handles, and bottoms of pieces. This beautiful glassware remained in production for three quarters of a century from 1912 to 1988. Corn Flower truly is an amazing story of longevity and success in the glass industry.

The Dufferin County Museum and Archives (DCMA) holds the largest public collection of Corn Flower glassware, with approximately 750 colored and clear glass pieces. The museum is home to the family and business archives of W.J. Hughes & Sons Corn Flower Limited, including several one-of-a-kind glassware pieces created by W.J. Hughes for family members and friends. The DCMA was kind enough to allow Walt Lemiski to bring several elusive pieces of Corn Flower to the studio in Pennsylvania for inclusion in this book. The enjoyment you receive from this chapter is due to their generosity and Walt's willingness to be the delivery person of DCMA glass, glassware from his private collection, and treasures from Canadian collectors Brenda Beckett and Brian J. Wing. (THANKS to all of you!)

If you are in the Toronto area be sure to include a visit to the Museum and Archives, and if you are unable to travel there it would be wonderful to send DCMA an e-mail or letter of appreciation for participating in this book.

Here are some particulars regarding the Dufferin County Museum & Archives: Museum staff, with the assistance of the Canadian Depression Glass Association and Pete Kayser, former company president, are in the process of identifying the many glass blanks on which Corn Flower was cut. Some archival materials, including photographs, are available for researchers' use.

An annual Corn Flower Festival takes place the second Sunday of June. Events include guest speakers, identification sessions, and a consignment sale of Corn Flower glassware. The DCMA is located at the intersection of Airport Road and Highway # 89 between Shelburne and Alliston, Ontario, Canada and is approximately one hour north of Toronto.

New donations of Corn Flower to the DCMA collection are always welcome. Please e-mail collectionsmanager@dufferinmuseum.com for more information.

There is an admission charge for adults and children over five. Hours may fluctuate by the season, so contact the DCMA for the particulars.

Contact Information:
Web Site: dufferinmuseum.com
E-mail: events@dufferinmuseum.com
Snail mail: P.O. Box 120
Rosemont, Ontario L0N 1R0 Canada
Toll Free 1.877.941.7787
or 1.705.435.1881
Fax: 1.705.435.9876

Unknown, 10.25" diameter. $25.
*Courtesy of Walt & Kim Lemiski –
Waltz Time Antiques.*

Unknown, 9.5" diameter. $25.
Courtesy of Brian J. Wing.

Duncan & Miller, 11" diameter with a
center foot. $55. *Courtesy of Brenda
Beckett.*

No. 281 by Imperial Glass Company, 13" diameter with a center foot. $65. *Courtesy of Brenda Beckett.*

Thought to be the
Princess blank by
Indiana Glass
Company, 11.25"
diameter with 5"
pedestal. $65.
Courtesy of Brian J.
Wing.

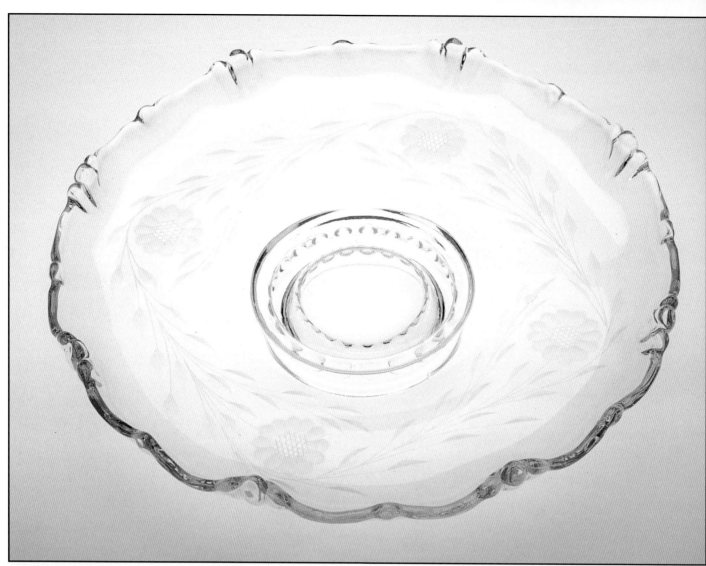

Indiana Glass Company, 12.5" diameter with a decorative foot. $30.
Courtesy of Walt & Kim Lemiski – Waltz Time Antiques.

Candlewick by Imperial Glass Company, 10"
diameter. $25. *Courtesy of Walt & Kim Lemiski –
Waltz Time Antiques.*

Candlewick by Imperial Glass
Company, 10" diameter with 3"
pedestal. $25. *Courtesy of
Brenda Beckett.*

Tear Drop by Duncan & Miller, 11"
diameter with a center foot. $55.
Courtesy of Brenda Beckett.

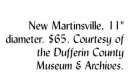

New Martinsville, 11"
diameter. $65. *Courtesy of
the Dufferin County
Museum & Archives.*

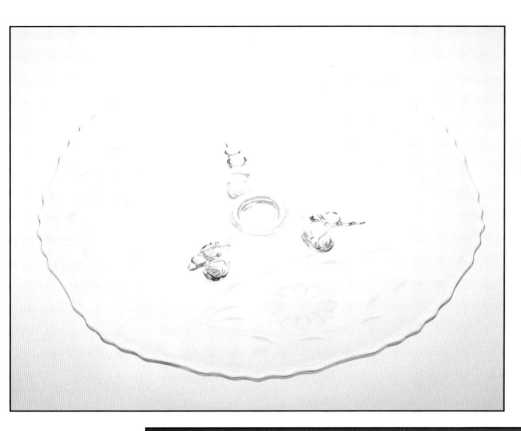

Unknown. 11" diameter with three feet. $30. *Courtesy of Walt & Kim Lemiski – Waltz Time Antiques.*

Tiffin, 10.75" diameter. $110. *Courtesy of the Dufferin County Museum & Archives.*

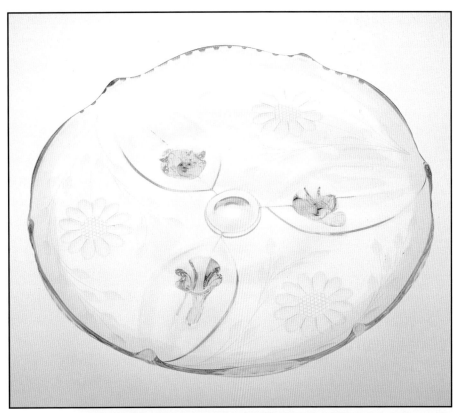

Lancaster Glass Company, 10.25" diameter. $150.
Courtesy of Brian J. Wing.

Lancaster Glass Company, 10.25" diameter.
$150. Courtesy of the Dufferin County Museum
& Archives.

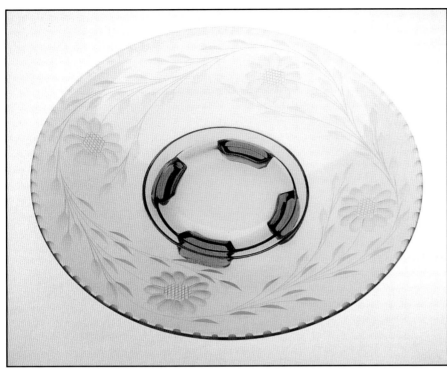

Unknown, 10.5" diameter with four toes. $175. *Courtesy of the Dufferin County Museum & Archives.*

United States Glass Company, 10.25" diameter with 2.25" pedestal. $200. *Courtesy of the Dufferin County Museum & Archives.*

Tiffin, 10.75" diameter. $175. Courtesy of the
Dufferin County Museum & Archives.

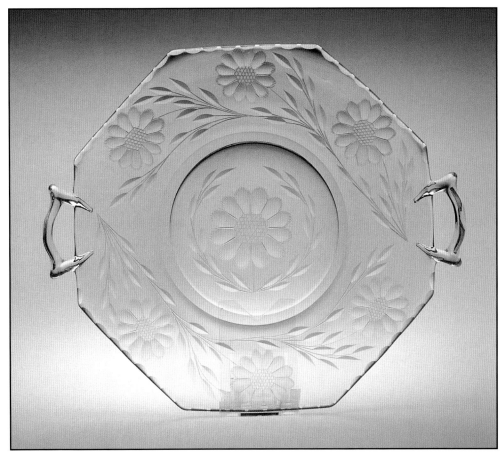

Heisey, 10.25" diameter. $185.
Courtesy of Brian J. Wing.

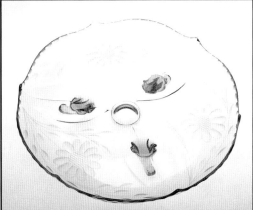

Lancaster Glass Company, 10" diameter with three feet. $175. *Courtesy of the Dufferin County Museum & Archives.*

Tiffin, 10.75" diameter. $175. *Courtesy of the Dufferin County Museum & Archives.*

Chapter Five

Depression Glass & Elegant Glass, Unknowns

There are some lovely cake plates with pattern names that are unknown to us. We have placed our contact information in the front of the book so let us know if you are able to provide additional information.

The arrangement of this chapter is by color, beginning with crystal (clear). As these are the "unknowns" no information on dates of production is provided. Some manufacturers are cited as characteristics seen on some of the glass indicate a strong likelihood of the producer.

Looking much like Imperial Glass Company's Candlewick, the 10.25" table on the 2.5" pedestal is molded in pie-shaped sections. $45. *Courtesy of Michelle Frazier.*

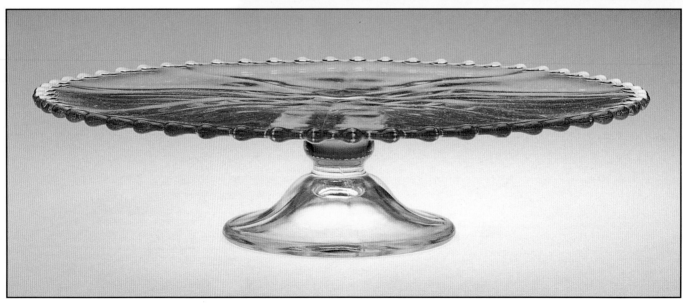

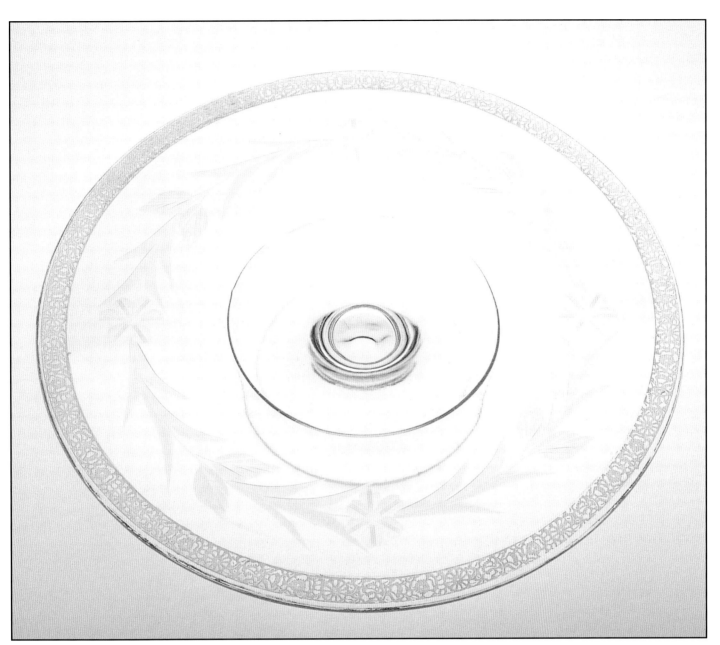

A half-inch gold band circles the 11" table. The pedestal is 2.25" tall. $30.

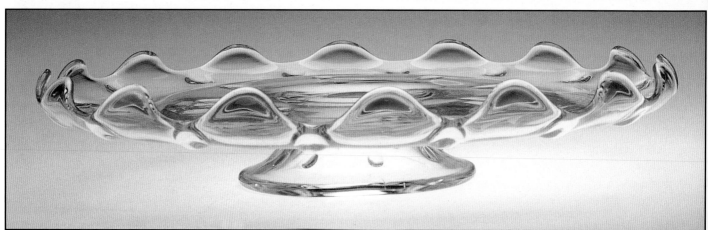

Flowers that resemble Lancaster Glass Company's Jubilee decorate a pedestal cake plate that features a decorative scallop and turned up rim. $35. *Courtesy of Michelle Frazier.*

Morning glories decorate the cover and three-toed base of this 12" diameter cake keeper. $50.

Both the 12" table and the base of the pedestal are decorated with tiny blossoms. The pedestal is 4" tall. $50. *Courtesy of Walt & Kim Lemiski – Waltz Time Antiques.*

A subtle optic is on the cover and the 11" base. The pedestal is 4" tall. $50. *Courtesy of Walt & Kim Lemiski – Waltz Time Antiques.*

This commonly seen cake plate is often paired with a Kromex lid. See Chapters Six and Seven for more information on Kromex and Kromex lids. $12.

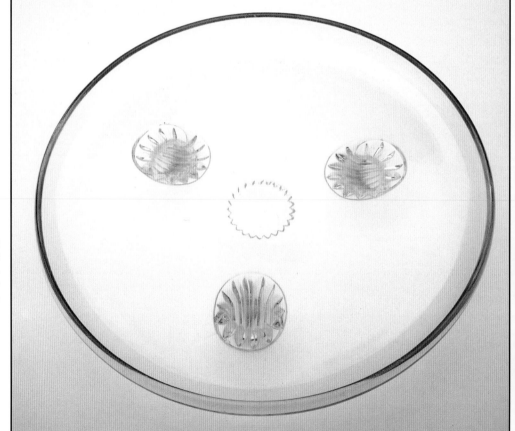

No design is on a 12.5" cake plate that has decorative curving feet thought to be made by Indiana Glass Company. $20. *Courtesy of Walt & Kim Lemiski – Waltz Time Antiques.*

106

The texture in the pie-shaped wedges is referred to as "Buttons and Bows" and was commonly used by many glass manufacturers since the late 1800s. It is not believed that this 10.5" diameter cake plate is that old. $35. *Courtesy of Walt & Kim Lemiski – Waltz Time Antiques.*

With characteristics of Avocado and Lily Pons, it is assumed that this 12.5" x 10.5" diameter cake plate with two handles was manufactured by Indiana Glass Company. $30. *Courtesy of Walt & Kim Lemiski – Waltz Time Antiques.*

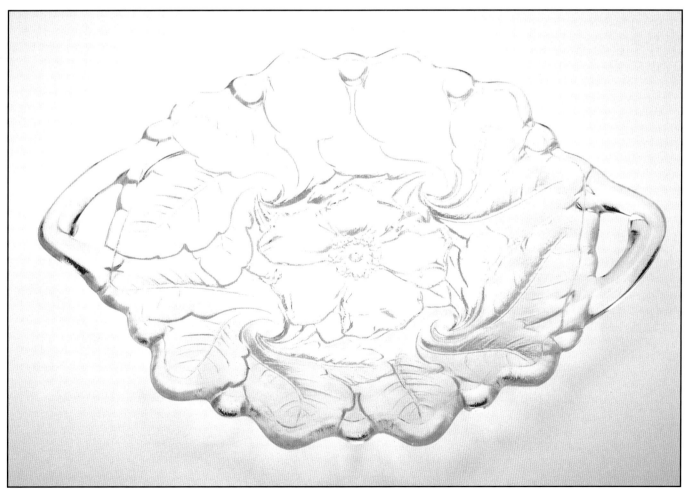

Thought perhaps to be Indiana Glass Company, this 13.25" cake plate features a silver overlay. $45. *Courtesy of Walt & Kim Lemiski – Waltz Time Antiques.*

Frosted with pastel blossoms, this 11.5" cake plate rests on three toes. $45.

Assumed to be a Lancaster Glass Company blank, this yellow cake plate is 10.25" in diameter. $25. *Courtesy of Norma Peacock/Peacock Antiques.*

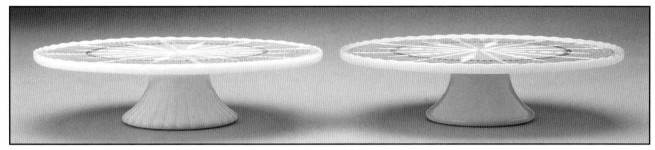

Made by Anchor Hocking, the name of these pedestal cake plates is unknown. Both are 10.25" in diameter with 2.5" pedestals. Found in ivory and white with gold trim these are believed to be from the 1950s. $15 each.

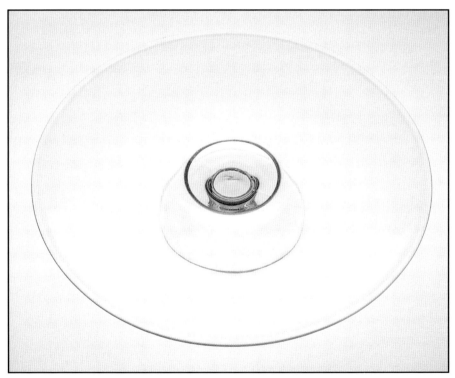

Pretty in pink, there is no information regarding this 10" cake plate. $35. *Courtesy of Walt & Kim Lemiski – Waltz Time Antiques.*

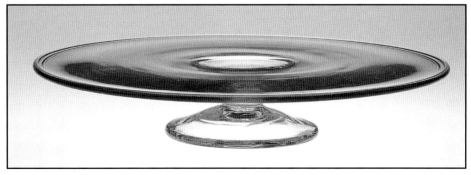

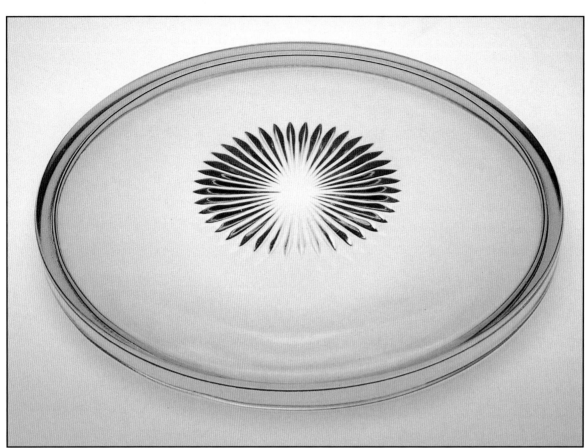

Thought to be United States Glass Company, this 9.75" diameter cake plate has a solid ring as its foot. $35. *Courtesy of Norma Peacock/Peacock Antiques.*

Nothing is known pertaining to this octagonal handled cake plate. $35. *Courtesy of Norma Peacock/Peacock Antiques.*

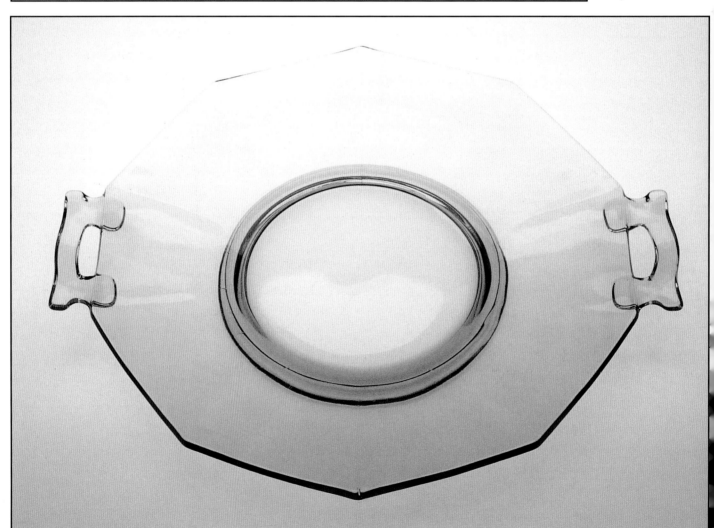

Sandra McPhee Stout discussed silver inlaid glass in *Depression Glass Number Two.* "'Puts the motion in your promotion,' according to the advertisement. *Silver Inlaid* was offered through tea and coffee outlets, sales contests, and other consumer deals. It combined two premium favorites, glass and silver. It was made in such colors as ruby red and topaz (silvered Iris and Herringbone Carnival lustre) by Century Metalcraft Corporation, and in ruby, blue, emerald, and amber with silver overlay by Cape Cod Art Glass Sales Company. These two companies were the two largest users of the silver inlay process on glass. Century Metalcraft was quite active in the premium sales promotion, stocking over 50 lines. Both companies bought glass blanks from contemporary glass factories, in addition to owning their own exclusive molds."[1]

[1]Sandra McPhee Stout, *Depression Glass Number Two* (Des Moines, Iowa: Wallace-Homestead Book Company), 36.

Silver inlaid brightens a ruby 13" diameter cake plate. $40.

Silver inlaid brightens a ruby 11.5" cake plate. $40 if perfect.

This red cake plate was lovely enough to be used on the cover, but there is no information available other than the size: 13.25" diameter with a center foot. $65. *Courtesy of Walt & Kim Lemiski – Waltz Time Antiques.*

No information is available for a 10.5" diameter cake plate with a center foot. $60. *Courtesy of Walt & Kim Lemiski – Waltz Time Antiques.*

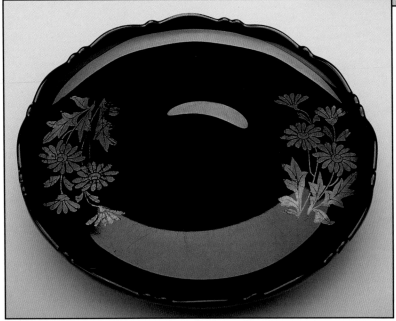

Looking very much like a piece of L.E. Smith glass, this 10" diameter cake plate with a 1.5" pedestal features silver overlay. $50. *Courtesy of Walt & Kim Lemiski – Waltz Time Antiques.*

Chapter Six

Post World War II

The end of the Second World War brought social and economic changes to the United States. To assist in the war effort women had entered the work force but the termination of the war didn't necessarily mean women returned to the role of full-time home-maker. Many women remained employed outside the home and at the end of a work-day were expected to perform all of the house-hold duties they did prior to becoming an employed individual. The passage of time only saw more women entering the workplace and many of these suffered an overwhelming sense of simply not being able to live up to the unrealistic expectations imposed by soci-etal pressures. It was not until the 1960s that American families began to evolve into husband and wife relationships that shared domestic responsibilities. However, from the late 1940s on, working women began to reevaluate their household tasks. Crocheting, embroidering, and baking became disposable activities. As home baking waned, manufac-turers produced fewer items that supported this endeavor, and this chapter is consider-ably shorter than previous ones for this rea-son.

During the war many factories were re-tooled to produce items needed for achiev-ing victory: grenades, shells, airplane parts, mess kits, and so on. In Chapter Seven, spe-cific information is provided on some of the manufacturers represented in this book and how they rose to meet the challenge of the war effort. Because manufacturers of metal products were highly profitable during World War II, they needed to generate a domestic demand for metal products as they returned to peacetime production. One of the results of this deliberate effort to create products that would be needed in American homes is the use of metal in kitchens. Everything from cabinets to cake carriers was available in metals and print ads attempted to persuade consumers that this was the "modern" way to decorate, store, and serve.

Sensitive to the evolving inclusion of metalware in the kitchen, manufacturers of glassware began to produce pieces that were compatible with the new trend. This chapter focuses on glass cake plates produced after the cessation of World War II. Glass manu-facturers created cake plates that were com-patible with a metal (or plastic) lid. The Anni-versary cake plate by Jeannette Glass Com-pany was made with plastic clips on the glass base to securely lock a cover in place. Other patterns featured an indented or raised ring near the outer rim perfect for the inclusion of a metal lid that could be bought sepa-rately. Kromex manufactured a "Kakover" lid that was to be added to a glass base one might already have in stock. Use of the term "three-toed" in the descriptions that follow is in reference to the design having three little feet (or toes) on the underside of the glass.

The end of the chapter features a look at post-war serving pieces and recipes.

The tag says it all: "Keeps Cake Fresh." Purchased at a five and dime store or a hardware store, a Kromex lid took a cake plate from merely serving to serving and storing, a modern idea indeed! *Courtesy of Janice Johnston / Behind the Green Door.*

Kromex lids were available with wood and plastic knobs. $8 each if in perfect (not dented) condition.

Basic clear glass cake plates became handy cake savers when covered. Each of the glass cake plates in the next section was manufactured with an elevated rim of glass to secure the lid. While not a portable unit, it was a clean, safe, fresh way to store cake within one's home.

This three-toed cake plate is reminiscent of Holiday by Jeannette Glass Company. $20.

This three-toed cake plate is reminiscent of Anniversary by Jeannette Glass Company. $20.

The three-toed cake plate shown here is quite common. $15.

A swirled edge provides decorative flare to this three-toed cake plate. $20.

Nothing says 1950s better than a touch of turquoise to the lid on a three-toed cake plate. $22. *Courtesy of Michelle Frazier.*

Here are cake plates from some familiar glass patterns of the post-war era. One of the details to be aware of is the evolution of color. Depression Glass and Elegant Glass cake plates are basically green, pink, crystal (clear), amber, and yellow. New times bring new colors: iridescent glass in a marigold color, fired-on colors, a greater use of crystal (clear), and in a hint of what was to come, avocado.

Anniversary by Jeannette Glass Company, 1947-1949, shown covered. Lid, $8; base, $8. *Courtesy of Michael Rothenberger / Mike's Collectibles.*

Anniversary by Jeannette Glass Company, 1947-1949, shown uncovered. Lid, $8; base, $8. *Courtesy of Michael Rothenberger / Mike's Collectibles.*

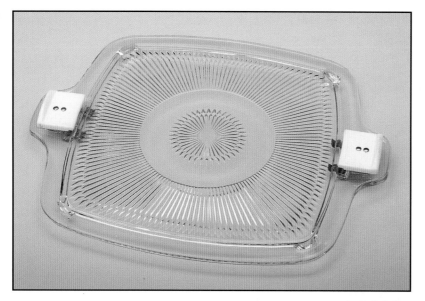

Anniversary by Jeannette Glass Company, 1947-1949. Lid, $15 (not shown); base, $30. Note the inclusion of tabs on the handles to secure a lid. *Courtesy of Walt & Kim Lemiski – Waltz Time Antiques.*

Camellia by Jeannette Glass Company, 1947-1951, 11" diameter. $20. *Courtesy of Walt & Kim Lemiski – Waltz Time Antiques.*

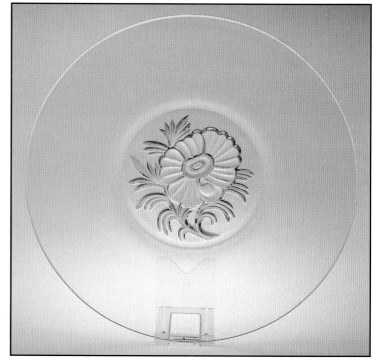

Early American Prescut by Anchor Hocking Glass, 13.5" diameter. $25. *Courtesy of Norma Peacock/Peacock Antiques.*

Emerald Crest by Fenton Art Glass Company. 13" diameter with pedestal shown on right. $125. *Courtesy of Doris McMullen.*

Floragold by Jeannette Glass Company, 1950s, 13.5" diameter. $25.

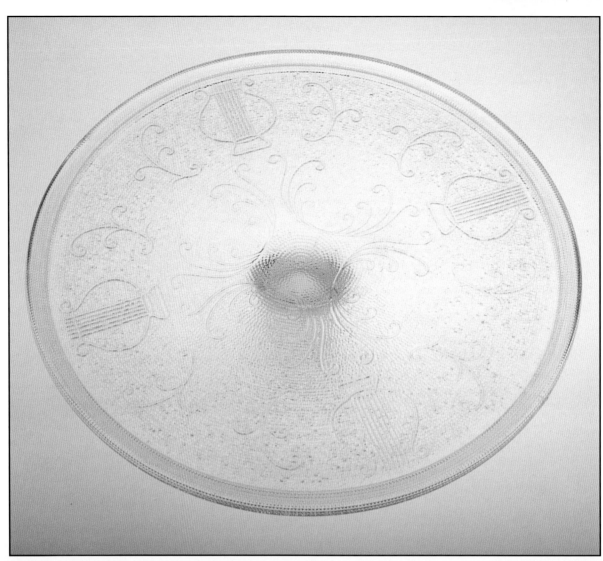

Harp by Jeannette Glass Company, 1954-1957, 10.25" diameter with
4.5" pedestal and no rim. $25. *Courtesy of David G. Baker.*

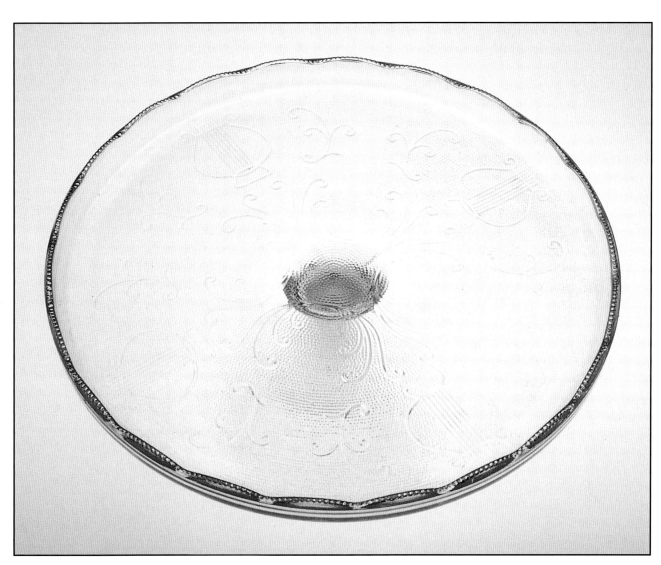

Harp by Jeannette Glass Company, 1954-1957, 10.25" diameter with 4.5"
pedestal and rim. $25. *Courtesy of Walt & Kim Lemiski – Waltz Time Antiques.*

Harp by Jeannette Glass Company, 1954-1957, 10.25" diameter with 4.5" pedestal in ice blue. $100. *Courtesy of Walt & Kim Lemiski – Waltz Time Antiques.*

Harp by Jeannette Glass Company, 1954-1957, 10.25" diameter with 5" pedestal. $50.

Heritage by Federal Glass Company, 1940-1955, 12" diameter. $15. *Courtesy of Walt & Kim Lemiski – Waltz Time Antiques.*

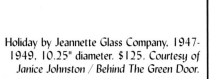

Holiday by Jeannette Glass Company, 1947-1949, 10.25" diameter. $125. *Courtesy of Janice Johnston / Behind The Green Door.*

Iris by Jeannette Glass Company, 1950 & 1969, 12" diameter. $35. Courtesy of Norma Peacock/Peacock Antiques.

Laurel (Gray) by Anchor Hocking Glass Corporation (Fire-King), 1950-1965. 11" diameter. $30. Courtesy of Michael Rothenberger / Mike's Collectibles.

Moderntone by Hazel-Atlas Glass Company, 1950s, 10.75" diameter. $20.

Moon and Stars by L.E. Smith, 1960s, 12" diameter with 1.75" pedestal. $35. *Courtesy of Michael Rothenberger / Mike's Collectibles.*

Swirl by Anchor Hocking Glass
Corporation (Fire-King), 1949-1962.
11" diameter. $30.

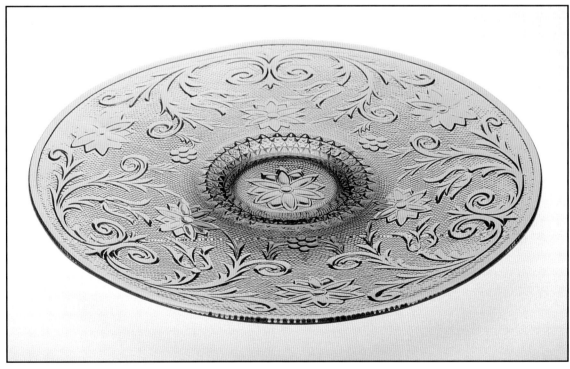

Tiara by Indiana Glass Company, 1970-1998,
12.75" diameter with 1.5" pedestal. $40.
*Courtesy of Michael Rothenberger / Mike's
Collectibles.*

White Hall by Indiana Glass Company, 1980s, 12" diameter with three toes. $35.

Here are some lovely serving pieces available to homemakers in the late 1940s and 1950s.

Hollow sterling silver handle with stainless steel blade in Princess pattern by International Silver Co. for Fine Arts Silver Co.; 1949. $20-25. *Courtesy of Les Fawber & Tom Dibeler / L.E. Fawber Antiques.*

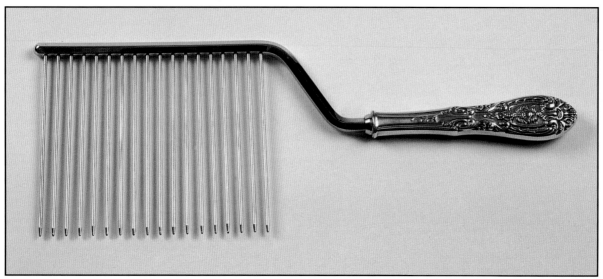

Hollow sterling silver handle with stainless steel teeth cake breaker in Crown Princess pattern by International Silver Co. for Fine Arts Silver Co.; 1949. $35-45. Note: Cake breakers with sterling silver handles are difficult to find. *Courtesy of Les Fawber & Tom Dibeler / L.E. Fawber Antiques.*

Sterling handle with stainless steel blade by S. Kirk & Son, Baltimore; circa 1950s. $35-45. Courtesy of Les Fawber & Tom Dibeler / L.E. Fawber Antiques.

Hollow sterling silver handle with stainless steel blade by S. Kirk & Son, Baltimore; circa 1950s. $20-25. Courtesy of Les Fawber & Tom Dibeler / L.E. Fawber Antiques.

Based on a recipe from the late 1950s, here is Spice Cake.

Spice Cake

3 cups flour

1 1/2 teaspoons baking soda

1 1/2 teaspoons cinnamon

3/4 teaspoon nutmeg

3/4 teaspoon cloves

3/4 cup melted shortening

1 1/2 cups buttermilk

3 large eggs

1 1/4 cups packed light brown sugar

1 cup granulated sugar

Grease two nine-inch layer pans. Thoroughly mix the dry ingredients. Add shortening and buttermilk and beat until smooth. In another bowl beat eggs and slowly add both sugars while still beating. Add the egg and sugar mixture to the dry ingredients and mix completely. Pour into pans and bake at 350 degrees for 35 to 40 minutes. Frost with:

Spice Cake, cont.

Frosting

2 egg whites

3/4 cup light brown sugar, packed

1/3 cup light corn syrup

2 tablespoons water

1/4 teaspoon cream of tartar

1 1/2 teaspoons vanilla

Combine all of the ingredients except for the vanilla in the top of double boiler. Cook and beat constantly while over boiling water until mixture forms peaks. Remove from heat and add vanilla. Beat until stiff enough to spread on spice cake.

Chapter Seven

Cake Carriers

Many of the companies that produced the metal and plastic cake carriers featured in this chapter have roots deep in the production industry of the early twentieth century. The first section of this chapter provides brief historical information on several of the companies whose wares are featured. I was unable to locate any pertinent information on Decoware and Kromex.

Everedy: The Lebherz brothers opened the Everedy Factory in Frederick, Maryland on December 27, 1923. Specializing in cooking utensils and gadgets, the first bottle capper patent was held by the Lebherz brothers. It was initially a huge success because of its usefulness in bottling homemade alcohol during the Prohibition era, but when Prohibition ended this item was no longer needed in any quantity. Up until the onset of World War II the Everedy Factory created pots, pans, and other kitchen items and were among the earliest of manufacturers to chrome-plate. Like many kitchenwares factories, the Everedy plant was temporarily retooled for the war effort; one of the most notable war items produced there was grenades. After more than four decades of being a major employer in Frederick, Maryland, the Everedy Company was purchased and then transferred to a new location where it continued production until its termination in 1977. Today Everedy Square, the original site of the factory, has been redeveloped for multiple uses.

Here is an advertisement for Everedy products. The $4.50 cake cover is shown with an Anniversary cake plate. Jeannette Glass Company produced Anniversary from 1947-1949 so one can assume this ad was from the late 1940s. *Courtesy of Janice Johnston / Behind the Green Door.*

This is the mark on the underside of the base.

A shiny chrome cake carrier is a signature Everedy piece. $30. *Courtesy of Janice Johnston / Behind the Green Door.*

J.L. Clark Manufacturing: John L. Clark of Rockford, Illinois invented the "Gem Flue Stopper" and created a manufacturing plant to produce it in 1904. The metal scraps were utilized for the manufacture of salve tins and this initiated consumers to J.L. Clark packaging. As explained on the J.L. Clark website (http://www.jlclark.com): "As business grew, new products were added and lithography became an essential part of the Clark business. Demand for their high-quality work led them to grow, and a new plant at the present location was completed Thanksgiving week, 1911." Today J.L. Clark is still expert in "metal decorating, fabricating, and plastic injection molding."

Kromex: Little is known other than the location of the factory: Cleveland, Ohio.

Lustro Ware/Columbus Plastic Products, Columbus, Ohio: There is little on record regarding this company other than an interesting story which follows: Reporter, novelist, script writer, publicist, and entertainer, Alma Sioux Scarberry, was hired by the Columbia Broadcasting System in Hollywood, California in 1940 as a publicity specialist and soon became head of the writing department at the Mutual Don Lee Network. She also composed many songs during the 1940s and 1950s. All of this exposure helped her create a network of friends in the entertainment industry. When she was hired in 1959 to do public relations for Columbus Plastic Products, Inc., in Ohio, Scarberry renewed her contacts in Hollywood and was able to market the company's Lustro Ware merchandise as several television variety shows and commercials used Lustro Ware products as props.

The Mirro Aluminum Company: The oldest company featured, The Mirro Company was established on May 10, 1897 by Jo-

seph Koenig in Two Rivers, Wisconsin under the name "Aluminum Goods Manufacturing Company." Contracts for cooking utensils, mess kits, and canteens for World War I troops provided employment opportunities, and in 1917 "Mirro" aluminum began to be nationally distributed. The Second World War resulted in rededicating production lines for the war effort, providing necessities as varied as airplane landing gear parts and canteens. In 1956 the Mirrocraft brand of boats was introduced and a year later the company name was changed to "Mirro Aluminum Company." Mirro is still manufacturing quality aluminum products although the boat division was sold to former employees in 1982 establishing Northport Incorporated while maintaining the Mirrocraft name.

This is the mark on the underside of the base.

It is rare to find an aluminum cake carrier with a wooden handle. Shown is "spun aluminum;" anodized aluminum is shown within this chapter. $25.

NESCO: The initials are an acronym for "National Enameling and Stamping Company" a subsidiary of the Metal Ware Corporation of Wisconsin, an early manufacturer of pots, pans, buckets, and farm accessories needed in rural Wisconsin. In the early 1930s several engineers at NESCO began experimenting with the newly available electricity and created a "portable oven." NESCO employees and employees of the local electric company went door to door throughout rural Wisconsin selling electric service, light bulbs, and NESCO electric ovens. NESCO was eventually split with products being purchased by a variety of manufacturers.

The West Bend Company: Bernhard C. Ziegler established the West Bend Aluminum Company on September 27, 1911. He and six other men each invested $1000 to incorporate this business that would provide employment for West Bend, Wisconsin citizens after a local pocketbook manufacturing company was destroyed in a fire. Earliest products included a variety of pans and a "water dipper." A variety of unique all-aluminum kitchen appliances were manufactured for more than twenty years. In 1933, West Bend's first copperware items were produced: pitchers, tumblers, trays, and mugs. These items were so successful The West Bend Company survived the Great Depression, a time when many companies failed. The onset of World War II compelled all aluminum to be directed toward the war effort and West Bend manufactured everything from cartridge cases to powder tanks. When the war ended, the company returned to the manufacturing of small appliances, cooking utensils, and giftware. In 1947 West Bend produced the first air-cooled outboard motor (later bought by Chrysler Corp.) and in 1951 their first stainless steel cooking utensils. In 1961 the company simplified its name to: "The West Bend Company" and continues today to be a vital leader in innovative small kitchen appliances.

A wooden acorn makes an unusual and decorative finial on this West Bend cake carrier. $25. Courtesy of Walt & Kim Lemiski – Waltz Time Antiques.

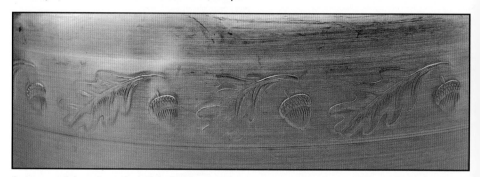

A close up of the embossed motif that circles the lid shows how appropriate the acorn finial actually is.

This is the mark on the underside of the base.

Caring for Your Cake Carrier

Caring for a cake carrier is quite simple. As most of these items were produced prior to dishwashers, hand washing is necessary to maintain bright colors and shine. Use nothing abrasive – no harsh detergents, no steel wool, no scrub-type sponges – on any surface. Abrasives will damage lithographs and scratch aluminum, chrome, and copper. We recommend washing gently with a grease-cutting detergent – never soaking in standing water for any time whatsoever – and a soft rag or sponge. To maintain a bright shine, dry immediately using gentle patting motions. Delicate drying is particularly important on these; rough handling can damage old lithographs. If you have sticker marks, try any goo-removing product, but not on clear plastic as these tend to make the plastic foggy.

An interesting website to visit is called "Kromex, or that wacky kitchenware" (www.uglx.org/kromex.html). One can learn in great detail how to repair a cake carrier. What follows is taken directly from this most insightful website:

"I bought one of the polished chrome cake keepers that matches the plastic-and-spun-aluminum canisters, but it was badly dented and scratched (it was also very cheap). Here's how I fixed it to a like-new condition.

"The first step was to get the dents out. My primitive technique was to use a small nail hammer, various diameters of dowel rod, and a curved surface that reasonably matched the curve of the lid. (The dents were in the top of the lid, so the curve wasn't that steep.) It was just a matter of hammering the dents from the inside of the lid until they came out; the dowel rod helped to make sure I wasn't hammering too large an area, and also softened the hammer a bit.

"That was the easy part, actually. The hard part was to get the scratches out, and then bring the top of the lid back to a mirror-like finish. The technique I described above (increasingly smaller grits of sandpaper followed by a buffing wheel) did the trick…it just takes a lot of elbow grease.

"The plastic portion of the lid was in good shape. I just needed to do a little bit of polishing, followed by repainting the letters with thinned Testors enamel."

To get the details on the "increasingly smaller grits of sandpaper followed by a buffing wheel" simply visit this website.

Valuing Your Cake Carrier

There are several design features worth noting that affect a carrier's value and usefulness. Cake (or food) carriers can have one, two, or three parts. A wire handle that applies enough pressure to maintain immobility holds multiple units together. Normally a carrier with several sections is designed to hold a cake and a pie or other item that has less height than the cake. Some lids simply touch the base; some lids fit into a groove in the base; some lids lock into the base with any number of configurations. Locking lids might gently turn into (as one would screw on a lid) a base or have clamps that catch and hold the lid. Again, a wire might be used to hold a lid in place while also providing a carrying handle. Earliest handles were metal wire or glass knobs.

Cake carriers were created in a variety of materials: tin, chrome, copper, aluminum, and plastic and with combinations of these.

The materials used on carriers reflect what was being manufactured at the time of production in respect to other kitchenwares. For instance, if Kromex produced spun aluminum cake carriers, they would have also been manufacturing spun aluminum canisters and shakers at the same time. Advertisements would have shown kitchens decorated with these matching pieces in an effort to entice the consumer into purchasing multiple pieces.

Ultimately the buyer and the seller determine value, but here are a few points to consider. The first, second, and third most important influences on value are: condition, condition, condition. Colorful cake carriers that were made with matching canisters, bread boxes, and so on are of the most value as they are in the highest demand by collectors decorating a kitchen. Many of these were produced by Decoware.

An advertisement for Decoware reminds the consumer that canisters are available to match the cake carrier. Most Decoware cake carriers have matching shakers, bread boxes, garbage pails, trash cans, wax paper holders, dust pans, and more! Decoware sets were produced since the 1930s and this advertisement is from the January 1951 issue of "Chatelaine," a Canadian magazine for women. *Courtesy of Walt & Kim Lemiski – Waltz Time Antiques.*

Like other areas of collecting, unique pieces also have a higher value, as do pieces that are cross-collectible. An example of this are the Scottie and Westie (Moxie!) cake carriers pictured in this chapter. These would be of interest to Scottie, Westie, and dog collectors and would command a higher price. Although many of these today have values of thirty dollars or more, in their day they were not expensive. In fact, for two orders of the magazine *The Farmer's Wife* in 1931 a cake carrier was free!

One of these attractive colors and decorations will be sent you.

It doesn't get any cheaper than free. Contemporary collectors place a great deal of value on items that were mass-produced and given away. It is difficult to expect such low-end merchandise to be free from imperfections. *Courtesy of Walt & Kim Lemiski – Waltz Time Antiques.*

Metal Cake Carriers

The Corningware Cornflower decorates this cake carrier with a locking lid and might be of interest to a collector with matching casseroles or other Corning products. $30. *Courtesy of Walt & Kim Lemiski – Waltz Time Antiques.*

The original intent of this two-part carrier was to enable a cake and a pie to have safe, easy transport. The stylized motif suggests the time of manufacture to be the late 1920s or early 1930s. The wire locks the two sections together and provides a handle. $35.

'The "Carlton" Cake Saver' has patent dates from 1930 and 1935. A wire keeps the lid secure while providing a handle. $30.

THIS SIDE DOWN
COVER RESTS ON OTHER SIDE

Unless assembled properly the air tight seal is not obtained and the portable handle cannot fit properly

THE "CARLTON" CAKE SAVER
Patents No. 1,762,417 – 2,009,516

This is the mark on the underside of the base.

The porcelain-knobbed lid sits on a base marked "this side up." Although some wear is evident, strawberries are a very popular kitchen theme and cake carriers reflecting this motif are rare. $40 as shown, more with improved condition.

The red plastic knobs are too little to perk up a rather dull cake carrier. Although this has two parts and retains as-new condition, most collectors would pass on this in favor of something with more flair. $20.

A fifties still life decorates a cake carrier with a copper pie section on top. The wire has evolved to hold the sections together and to provide a separate handle for more comfort during periods of mobility. $30.

A variation on a theme, this carrier is the same as the previous one except for an additional copper pie section below. Both seem to be "Peoria" products but are unmarked. $35.

This "TRIPLE DECK FOOD CARRIER" by Peoria still has the original box. Little is known of the Peoria Metal Specialty Company other than it was located in Peoria, Illinois. Newer carriers were called "food" carriers for broader acceptance by modern, working women. $25 without box, add $10 for the box.

The barbecue chef is delighted with the Scottie as shown on this two part carrier. $40 as shown with some wear, more with improved condition. *Courtesy of Walt & Kim Lemiski – Waltz Time Antiques.*

Embossed utensils wrap around in a very fifties motif. This lid does not lock into place making this a cake keeper (to keep or protect the cake) rather than a cake carrier. $25. *Courtesy of Walt & Kim Lemiski – Waltz Time Antiques.*

This is the mark on the underside of the base.

The plain metal top of the lid can also be found in white or red. A match safe and canisters were also made with this floral and wheat motif. This is unmarked but definitely resembles Decoware designs. $15 as shown, $30 with color on the top of the lid. *Courtesy of Walt & Kim Lemiski – Waltz Time Antiques.*

Shown is the cake carrier lid to "The Lady at the Gate" design found on many metal kitchen items. $35, if complete. *Courtesy of Janice Johnston / Behind the Green Door.*

Matching canisters are available in this very elusive motif. $30.

Checked bows were such a successful theme that glass companies and enamelware factories also produced items so decorated. Matching canisters are available in this charming Decoware design that is still very popular with collectors. $30. *Courtesy of Michelle Frazier.*

Gardening motifs are very popular at this time. This "flower cart" design is found on a plethora of additional metalware: canisters, breadbox, garbage pail, and more. The lid does not lock into the base, so to be accurate this is a cake keeper. $35.

This is another design that can be found with many matching pieces. The spray of flowers and polka dot background add bold color to any kitchen. A gentle turn of the lid locks this securely into the base. $35.

Exotic Anthurium were used on many kitchen items in the 1940s. Dinnerware, glasses, and more were produced with this bold blossom. Decoware's design features three metal hooks to secure the lid and base. $30. *Courtesy of Walt & Kim Lemiski – Waltz Time Antiques.*

There are many matching kitchen items with this Amaryllis design. Although unmarked, it seems to be a Decoware piece complete with a locking lid. $35.

Rose designs are frequently seen in vintage kitchenware, but this one is quite elusive. Found in Canada, it may have had little or no distribution in the United States. $35. *Courtesy of Walt & Kim Lemiski – Waltz Time Antiques.*

Personal bias allows us the privilege to say that however pleased the chef was to see the Scottish Terrier pictured earlier in this chapter, he is even more thrilled to see the West Highland White Terrier! $65.

Representing the 1960s, this avocado green three-part carrier will match few contemporary kitchens. $15.

Found in a rainbow of colors, this anodized aluminum piece is one of the largest carriers found measuring a full fourteen inches in diameter while most are about eleven to twelve inches. Let there be no doubt that this was for cake, as it is so marked. Labeling metal kitchenware as shown here was common in 1950s and 1960s design. $35. *Courtesy of Michael Rothenberger / Mike's Collectibles.*

Hand painted embellishments add charm to an otherwise uninteresting two part cake carrier. The glass knob helps to date this as one of the earliest examples in this chapter. The wire handle should rest on top of the glass knob, but a previous owner altered the design, perhaps to diminish the amount of tension on the wire thus easing its use. Age is not a huge factor in value, appearance is. This will have minimal appeal to today's buyers. $15. *Courtesy of Walt & Kim Lemiski – Waltz Time Antiques.*

Marked NESCO, this cake carrier was made in yellow, blue, and red. All colors have matching canisters and match safes. $25.

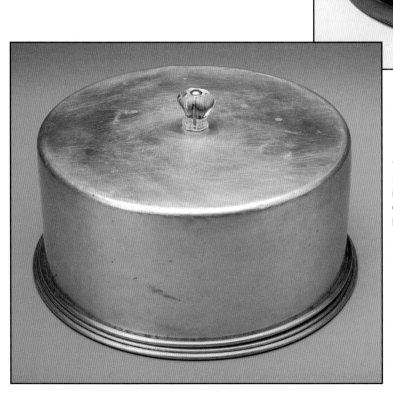

The green glass knob nicely mimics the green color on the aluminum lid creating a carrier that will match jade-ite kitchens. Because of the great coloration this is more desirable than many other cake carriers with an equally plain design. $25. *Courtesy of Michelle Frazier.*

This is the mark on the underside of the base.

The lithograph is quite worn on this tin cake saver that is among the oldest presented. The Asian-like design will have limited appeal. $15.

Three metal hooks secure the top and bottom of this Ballonoff cake carrier featuring unpopular colors that suppress its value. $15.

This is the mark on the underside of the base.

Nothing says 1960s more than mushrooms on kitchenware. Decoware's all-metal carrier was produced in a time when many consumers were purchasing plastic. $20.

This is the mark on the underside of the base.

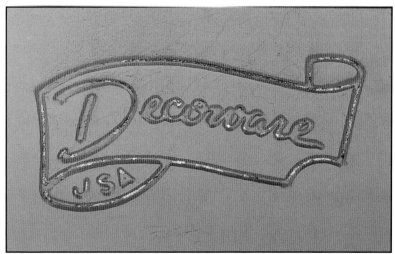

Hand painted blossoms decorate a cake carrier with a plastic handle. $20. *Courtesy of Walt & Kim Lemiski – Waltz Time Antiques.*

The floral design shown here was seen on a white cake carrier earlier in this chapter. Less popular in white, the fifties yellow will have a much greater demand and the two sections will come in handy. $30.

Square cake carriers were not seen before the end of the 1940s. Yellow with chrome indicate this was produced in the late 1950s. Tabs on the base slide back and forth to lock and unlock the lid. $35.

These daisies were also made in turquoise and appear to be Decoware in origin. Many matching accessories are available including canisters and a match safe. The lid locks by rotating it slightly. $35.

The anodized aluminum lid and base are secured with sliding tabs located on the base. $35. *Courtesy of Michael Rothenberger / Mike's Collectibles.*

West Bend copper kitchenware is becoming extremely popular. Here is the round cake carrier with a locking lid. As the twentieth century progressed portions of food increased. Early dinnerware featured dinner plates often smaller than nine inches in diameter, entirely too small by current standards. This cake carrier and its mate shown in the next picture are the two largest examples shown as each is 14.5" in diameter – truly reflecting contemporary standards in portion size. $30.

Square cake carriers are uncommon, but West Bend produced both round and square as shown here. A large assortment of matching kitchen items is available in either graphic. $30. *Courtesy of Walt & Kim Lemiski – Waltz Time Antiques.*

Look for the West Bend name on the handle.

Although there are no bold primary colors in this motif, the charming scene more than compensates. $30.

Hand painted flowers add color to an otherwise uninteresting yet early cake carrier. The glass knob and wire closure indicate this is probably from the early 1930s. $15.

An intricate silhouette motif is punctuated with bright colors on this lid. Found in Canada, it is assumed but not confirmed that matching kitchenware was produced. $35, if complete. *Courtesy of Walt & Kim Lemiski – Waltz Time Antiques.*

Found (rarely) in turquoise and black, this is one of Decoware's most frequently seen pink designs in matching canisters. Pink cake savers are not plentiful as, although the color was heavily promoted in the mid-1950s, it did not gain widespread acceptance. $30. *Courtesy of Michelle Frazier.*

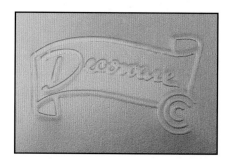

This is the mark on the underside of the base.

Peoria's "ALL PURPOSE FOOD CARRIER"
still has the original box. Little is known of
the Peoria Metal Specialty Company other
than it was located in Peoria, Illinois.
Newer carriers were called "food" carriers
for broader acceptance and thus use by
modern, working women. $25 without
box, add $10 for the box.

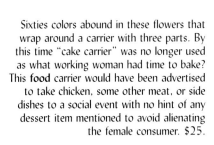

Sixties colors abound in these flowers that
wrap around a carrier with three parts. By
this time "cake carrier" was no longer used
as what working woman had time to bake?
This **food** carrier would have been advertised
to take chicken, some other meat, or side
dishes to a social event with no hint of any
dessert item mentioned to avoid alienating
the female consumer. $25.

153

A charming Pennsylvania Dutch motif decorates a Kromex cake carrier dated 1975. Two plastic handles secure the lid to the base. $20.

A closer view shows the date of manufacture.

Done in "Early American" colors, the flowers do little to perk up the overall look of this ATAPCO cake carrier. The plastic base has two latches to hold the metal lid in place. $15.

This is the mark on the underside of the base.

Measuring 15" x 11.5" this is the only rectangular cake carrier we have seen. Not only practical for sheet cake, it is particularly interesting as it features an advertisement on the metal lid that locks into the plastic bottom. One might assume that the carrier held A.K. Bernhard cake and was a bonus when a purchase was made. $30.

155

Plastic Cake Carriers

Plastic cake carriers are rarely seen for two reasons. First, they had a tendency to crack when used, so much of what was produced has not survived. More importantly, plastic kitchenware was introduced after World War II, primarily in the 1950s. By this time many women were working and the notion of Mother baking for the church bazaar, the family, or the neighbors was quickly vanishing.

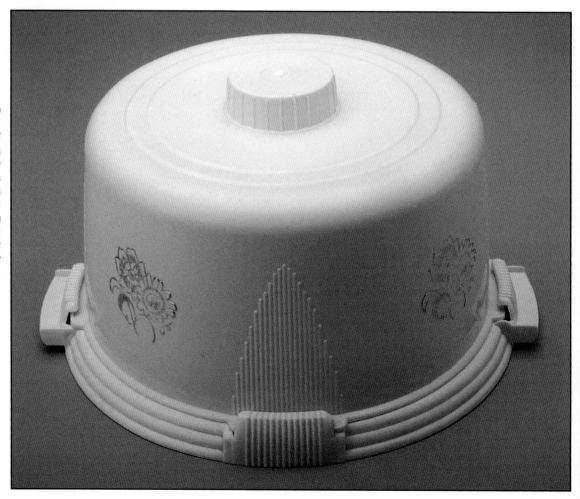

This is the mark on the underside of the base.

Lustro-Ware is one of the most popular manufacturers with today's collectors. Known for creating brightly colored utensils, canisters, and more, it seems odd to find a cake saver in this neutral tone. Tabs designed in the handles secured the lid to the base. The value shown is because this is a Lustro-Ware item. $30.

This is the 'NO. 600 "LOCKLIFT" CAKE COVER" by the Trans. Spec. Co. of Cleveland, Ohio and features an ingenious four-way locking system that insures security when food was transported. The patent number 2637617 is from 1953 validating the fact that most plastic kitchenware was from the 1950s. $15.

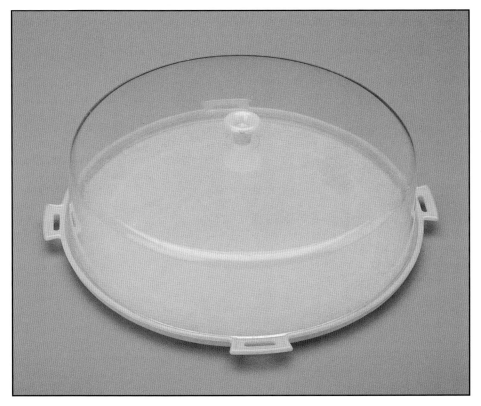

In reality, this 1950s item was marketed as a pie carrier as it is not tall enough to hold a layer cake though a single layer would be fine. Rarely seen in any condition, a perfect carrier as shown is a prize for collectors of plastic kitchen items. $30. *Courtesy of Michelle Frazier.*

Now that we have worked our way well into the 1950s let's have a final look at a recipe from this era and serving pieces of the next decade. The fact that this is a no-bake cake that is prepared a day in advance reflects the need of working women to simplify cooking from scratch. Today we realize it can be unsafe to consume raw eggs.

Refrigerator Cake

2 sticks softened butter
2 1/2 cups 10x sugar
4 eggs, separated
1 8-ounce can crushed pineapple, well drained
1 square unsweetened chocolate, melted

1 1/2 teaspoons vanilla extract
About 18 ladyfingers, split lengthwise
1/2 cup miniature chocolate chips (Barbara prefers semi-sweet)

Day before:

Thoroughly blend butter with sugar until very light and fluffy. Add egg yolks one at a time mixing completely each time. In another bowl beat

Refrigerator Cake, cont.

egg whites until stiff and add to butter mixture. Divide this into 3 equal parts in three different bowls. Add pineapple to one, add melted chocolate to one, and add vanilla to one. Line bottom of 10" x 6" x 2" baking dish with one third of split ladyfingers; pour on pineapple mixture. Cover with another third of ladyfingers and spread with chocolate mixture. Cover with last third of ladyfingers and spread on vanilla mixture. Refrigerate 24 hours.

Before serving:

Sprinkle cake with miniature chocolate chips and cut into squares. If knife gets messy, wipe between cuttings. Garnish with whipped cream if desired.

157

Silver plate cake server with stainless steel blade. Unknown manufacturer, circa 1960s. $10-12. *Courtesy of Les Fawber & Tom Dibeler / L.E. Fawber Antiques.*

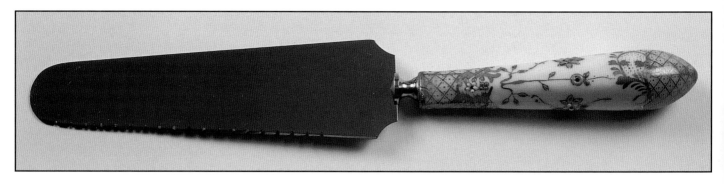

China handle with enamel floral motif. English, circa 1960. $20-25. *Courtesy of Les Fawber & Tom Dibeler / L.E. Fawber Antiques.*

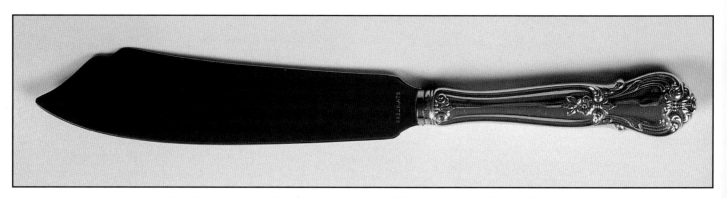

Silver plate cake server with stainless steel blade by William Rogers & Son, Meriden, Connecticut; circa 1960s. $10-12. *Courtesy of Les Fawber & Tom Dibeler / L.E. Fawber Antiques.*

If you love dessert as much as we, than you may internalize this statement much deeper than many: "Baking is an art – you are the artist. The material of this art are such common things as eggs, flour, and sugar. The brush is a mixing spoon and the canvas is, of course, your dinner table."[1]

Art was meant to be enjoyed! We're not just talking dessert here. We have learned that a great deal of thought and energy goes into making a lovely table for your friends or family to enjoy. Think of your table as a still life, a work of art. Then consider how much better everything looks on a cake plate!

"No meal, we feel, is complete without the dessert (as any member of your family will agree). But how to choose from so many delectable recipes? The rule is simple: Keep the rest of the meal in mind when you plan its finale. If the meal is light, a hearty dessert is right. If the weather is hot, a hot dessert is not. Is the meal short on starchy food? Then a pudding or cake-dessert is good. And if it's company you expect – a super, dazzling dessert creation is correct."[2]

So, all you dessert aficionados, live, laugh, love, and pass the cake!

[1]General Foods Kitchens, *All About Baking* (New York: Random House, Inc.), 1.
[2] Good Housekeeping, *Good Housekeeping's Dreamy Desserts* (Chicago, Illinois: Consolidated Book Publishers) 2, 5-6.

Bibliography

Andersen, Charlotte C. "Depression Recipes Which Aren't Depressing." *Women's Circle Home Cooking*. House of White Birches, Inc./Tower Press, May 1984.

Bartlett, John. *Familiar Quotations*. Boston: Little, Brown and Company, 1992.

Berolzheimer, Ruth. *250 Classic Cake Recipes*. Chicago, Illinois: Consolidated Book Publishers, Inc., 1940.

General Foods Kitchens. *All About Baking*. New York: Random House, 1960.

General Foods Kitchens. *All About Home Baking*. New York: Random House, 1936.

Good Housekeeping. *Good Housekeeping's Dreamy Desserts*. Chicago, Illinois: Consolidated Book Publishers, 1967.

Grace Methodist Episcopal Church. *Our Choicest Recipes*. Utica, NY: T.J. Griffiths, 1897.

Mauzy, Barbara & Jim. *Mauzy's Depression Glass, 3rd Edition*. Atglen, PA: Schiffer Publishing, Ltd., 2004.

Stout, Sandra McPhee. *Depression Glass Number Two*. Des Moines, Iowa: Wallace-Homestead Book Company, 1971.

Townsend, Wayne. *Corn Flower*. Winnipeg, Manitoba, Canada: Hignell Printing Limited, 2001.

250 Delectable Dessert Recipes. Chicago, Illinois: Consolidated Book Publishers, 1949.

Walk, John. *The Big Book of Fenton Glass 1940-1970*. Atglen, PA: Schiffer Publishing, Ltd., 1998.

Weatherman, Hazel Marie. *Colored Glassware of the Depression Era 2*. Ozark, MO: Weatherman Glassbooks, 1974.

Resources

http://magazines.ivillage.com/countryliving/collect

www.dgshopper.com

www.glass-time.com

www.jlclark.com/company.htm

www.nesco.com/about/

www.RootsWeb.com/th/read/MDFREDER/2000-12/0977929094

www.system.missouri.edu

www.taurasos.com/history.html

www.uglx.org/kromex

www.westbend.com/westbend/
    catalog.cmf?dest=dir&link=section&linkon=section&linkid=16